OUT ON A LIMB

Happy BIRTHDAY, LIETH !

Hugs,

OUT ON A LIMB

SERMONS OF RISK AND REVOLUTION

Glenna Shepherd

Grateful acknowledgment is made for permission to reproduce copyright material from the following works:

Strength of the Weak, Dorothee Soelle (Westminster John Knox). *Unexpected News: Reading the Bible with Third World Eyes*, Robert McAfee Brown (Westminster). "The Road Not Taken," Robert Frost, *Mountain Interval* (Henry Holt). *Pacific Edge: Three Californias*, Kim Stanley Robinson (Orb). "Letter from Birmingham Jail," Martin Luther King, *Why We Can't Wait* (Penguin): reprinted by arrangement with The Heirs to the Estate of Martin Luther King Jr., c/o Writers House as agent for the proprietor, New York, NY, © 1963 Dr. Martin Luther King, Jr., © renewed 1991 Coretta Scott King. *The Cancer Journals*, Audre Lorde (Aunt Lute). "For Those Tears I Died," Marsha Stevens, *I Still Have a Dream* CD (BALM). *Suffering*, Dorothee Soelle (Fortress). "Faith and Patriotism", Charles J. Chaput, from *The New York Times*, October 22 © 2004 *The New York Times*; all rights reserved; used by permission and protected by the Copyright Laws of the United States; the printing, copying, redistribution, or retransmission of this content without express written permission is prohibited. "In Her Own Image," Deena Metzger, *Heresies*. *Against the Wind: Memoir of a Radical Christian*, Dorothee Soelle (Augsburg Fortress). "I Sing a Song of the Saints of God," Lesbia Scott, *Everyday Hymns for Little Children* (The Society of Saints Peter and Paul): © 1929 Morehouse Publishing Group (Church Publishing Group, Inc). *Twelve Steps and Twelve Traditions*, Alcoholics Anonymous World Service.

Every effort has been made to trace copyright holders. The publisher would be grateful to be notified of any omissions, which will be rectified in future editions.

First published in 2015 by Tollington Press, Machynlleth, Wales, UK
www.tollingtonpress.co.uk

Cover design by jenksdesign@yahoo.co.uk
Typeset by Helen Sandler

Printed in the United States of America by
Atlanta Book Printing on FSC-certified paper
www.atlantabookprinting.com

Contents

THE SUNDAYS AFTER PENTECOST

Foreword

by Rep. John Lewis

OUT ON A LIMB: Sermons of Risk and Revolution is much more than an inspiring devotional guide. It is a call to bring the rich spiritual symbols and meaning of the scriptures to bear on the social, political, and religious problems of our day. Its lineage connects to the social gospel, now revered but controversial at its birth, preached by Martin Luther King Jr., Walter Rauschenbusch, Reinhold Niebhur, Jim Lawson, Howard Thurman and others.

They were among the great theologians and thinkers whose ideas helped to frame the philosophical foundation of the Civil Rights Movement. Most do not perceive that, at its core, the movement was an invitation for spiritual revival in America led by ministers who used non-violent activism as a way to demonstrate the link between morality and justice. Their activism was an extension of their faith, as this book suggests.

We saw non-violent resistance as an action of love, meant to demonstrate the wise mandate God has given us to love even in the face of hate. We believed that every single human being was a spark of the divine and no law, no government, no church, no entity or person had a right to scar or damage that spark. That is the core principle of reconciliation, which believes the truth of human unity is eternal and irrevocable.

In the end, we believed love would have the final say. So our activism was a method we used to prick the conscience of a sleeping nation, and ignite the divine spark of our attackers, to remind them of the truth of human unity, already and eternally written on their hearts.

Our protests were designed to make this truth plain and reveal the mockery and injustice of existing law. We staged protests, disobeying laws that violated human integrity and denied the divinity of all life. We wanted to redeem the soul of America and grab it out of the jaws of moral demise by standing on our faith and demonstrating the need for ethical reparation.

Through this publication of her sermons, the Reverend Glenna Shepherd seeks to continue this conversation in her own way. Her contention that a rich inner life naturally leads to involved, passionate engagement with the suffering of the world is an extension of this philosophy. For the faithful to exercise a love that frees and heals others provides a direct link to the movement's social justice legacy.

If you believe that the central purpose of the life of Jesus Christ – the Great Teacher – was to demonstrate the way to liberate all humankind, you will be edified and inspired by this work. You will finish it firmly convinced that the faithful must do all that we can to bring equality and justice, love and freedom to this nation, to the world, and to our own souls.

Introduction

SOME OF MY earliest memories are memories of sermons: the tone, the actual words, the effect, and my subsequent reflections on and applications of the preacher's message. From around the age of six, sermons drew me to God, to the church, and to the art of preaching. The first preachers in my life, the Reverend Dr. Ralph L. Murray, minister at Smithwood Baptist Church, and the Reverend Dr. Charles S. Bond, senior pastor of Central Baptist Church of Fountain City – both in Knoxville, Tennessee – blended astute, probing biblical scholarship with a call to personal commitment and a life of faithful service. Their preaching stirred my heart and quickened my theological curiosity. I am grateful for such admirable role-models so early in my life.

Preaching, of course, is an in-the-moment event. Sermons are written for specific congregations at specific points in time. But hopefully the reader of collections such as this can resonate with these particular stories and situations and find some transferable insight in these applications of scripture. In this way, perhaps, a transient sermon can become literature, with the possibility of speaking to other people, times, and places.

Most every beginning preacher learns that no single sermon can say or do everything that is prompted by the scriptural text.

Entire books have been written on many of these lectionary passages. Rather, the sermon-writer finds the intersections of the text, the current climate of the world or the community, and the call to personal spiritual engagement. So, although this book is subtitled *Sermons of Risk and Revolution*, implying a social and political agenda, each sermon also reflects the biblical emphasis on personal faith and the mystical nature of both a spiritual life and the messages of scripture.

Any preacher's social location inevitably influences both our engagement of scripture and the applications of the scriptures with and for our congregations. So, a word about mine: I grew up in Southern Appalachia, in a home with two parents. In both home and church, the guiding values were service to others that flows from religious commitment; education; and following the mainstream, middle-class, Southern Baptist way of life and faith. The brand of Southern Baptist Church in which I grew up was not extremist. Rather, its preachers and teachers presented a rational form of piety with a clear call to ethical, faith-guided living. Sermons and Sunday School invited us, even as children and young people, to explore and question our faith. But church was not the beginning of my spiritual life. I have early memories of God, of mystical encounters and conversations that formed the bedrock on which my faith is grounded.

During my first career, as a musician, I was employed by congregations and schools that span American denominations: Catholic, United Methodist, Anglican, Presbyterian, Baptist, and Lutheran. The experiences that created this ecumenical résumé have contributed to my repertoire of theologies and liturgies and have, undoubtedly, shaped my preaching. That's a bit of my social and religious history.

But, perhaps just as importantly, my preaching is informed by my gender and sexual orientation. I read the scripture and hear the messages of the prophets and the life of Jesus as a woman and as a lesbian. I would go beyond claiming an understanding of *the social gospel* and say that I experience the scriptures as both fully social and fully personal.

Experiences with congregations in Europe and Africa have contributed to my reading of scripture and to my view of the place of the church in the world. This international work has led me to ask – in both my preaching and in my role as pastor – hard but essential questions about the future of the church. I am convinced that we, the church, must pay attention to the state of the world and allow current issues and thought to encounter and shape our religion. In fact, I see this as a privileged opportunity, an opportunity to apply the way of life that Jesus showed us and the biblical portrayal of the ever-new love of God to our rapidly changing world. We have a window of opportunity to bring grace, hope, equity, and the way of peace – if we dare to reimagine and reconstruct the church for today's world.

The church, in the form that we have known it in the past, is no longer viable. We must renew our mission, not only envisioning new strategies, but imagining and embracing new perspectives of God, new ways of spiritual engagement, worship, and service. The form of church of the future will certainly be different, and I suspect that the content will be as well, as we attend to the realities of religious pluralism and secularism. This means, I believe, hearing and appropriating the essential, life-giving messages of the gospel for a new age, addressing the longings, needs, and questions that are current and compelling.

And the prophets and Jesus have plenty to say about social and economic maladies. If we listen to their messages for our own time and dare to speak those still-revolutionary truths from the margins of the church and the world, perhaps the Spirit will stir in and through us.

The sermons included in this collection were written in a number of places for several congregations and gatherings. Most were preached in the context of churches I have served as pastor: Christ Covenant (Decatur, GA), Tampa, All God's Children (Minneapolis), and Portland (OR) – all part of Metropolitan Community Churches – and the Cathedral of Hope (Dallas) and Decatur (GA) United Churches of Christ. Others were written for larger conferences and gatherings in the UK, the US, and South Africa.

So, developing sermons in each particular social, religious, and community context has become for me a primary spiritual practice, a way of asking essential, timely questions of the texts. My process includes continually questioning the relevance of the texts them-selves. Do the stories and sayings of the scriptures have wisdom, insight, strength and hope to offer us? I have found much to commend them to us if we will dare to hear and heed their messages of risk and revolution, if we can grasp their radical messages about power: God's and ours.

My hope is that these sermons reflect that relevant and holistic way of life; that they, both in their real-time delivery and in this collection, present the revolutionary religion of the prophets and Jesus to which so many courageous men and women have given their lives. I hope that, in some small way, they are witness to the continuing relevance of the Christian life and a call to travel that mystical, connected, bold path of risky activism that is fueled by compassion and still holds the possibility of turning the world toward love, justice, and peace.

I am grateful to the preachers who have inspired my faith and my vocation through the years; to feminist, liberal, and liberation-ist theologians who have influenced my thought and have fired my conscience; and to ministerial friends and colleagues with whom I am privileged to share life and ideas, struggles and blessings. The faithfulness of these colleagues inspires and challenges me daily: faithfulness to authentic preaching and speaking, to ongoing spiritual discovery and scholarship, and to staying current on the political and social issues to which a relevant faith must speak.

I am also grateful to the congregations I've served. You have helped me keep my engagement of scripture applicable and current by sharing your lives, your hopes and fears, with me. My self-avowed secular friends, too, keep me attentive to the important questions about the relevance of the texts and the faith. My preaching would be impoverished without your presence in my life.

Glenna Shepherd, Atlanta, Georgia, 2014

A Note on the Text

BIBLE QUOTATIONS, unless otherwise noted, are from *The New Oxford Annotated Bible with Apocrypha, New Revised Standard Version* (New York: Oxford University Press, 2001).

I have inclusified the texts, usually using gender-neutral language for God. Most of us would agree that God is without gender, but the actual word *God* implies masculinity. To place less emphasis on any gender assignment for God, I have avoided pronouns – either male or female. Feminist theologians and biblical scholars have written extensively on this subject; so, the reader can find a plethora of resources for further reading. *Inclusive Language in the Church* by Nancy A. Hardesty presents an excellent introduction to both the theory and practice.

Where I quote from other works, these are listed in full in the Bibliography at the end.

ADVENT

1

SUBVERSIVE PRAISE

Luke 1:46b-55

And Mary said, "My soul magnifies God, and my spirit rejoices in Yahweh my Savior,
who has looked with favor on the lowliness of this servant.
Surely, from now on all generations will call me blessed;
for the Mighty One has done great things for me, and holy is God's name.
Divine mercy is for those who fear God from generation to generation.

God has shown strength with that holy arm, has scattered the proud in the thoughts
   of their hearts,
brought down the powerful from their thrones, and lifted up the lowly;
God has filled the hungry with good things, and sent the rich away empty."

☙

I REMEMBER MARY.

In fact, I remember two Marys from my childhood. I can see the Catholic Mary at our community hospital, St. Mary's: her statues were prominent in corridors and in the manicured gardens that surrounded the hospital buildings. Her picture hung starkly over each bed, as she offered prayers for the sick. This Mary was treated as "other" by the more evangelical folks in the community.

She was considered an idol, a perversion, or at least a misrepresentation of the silent, faceless, necessary vessel, the Mother of Jesus.

The Baptist Mary, the "correct" Mary in my family, was visible only in Nativity scenes and on Christmas cards. Oh, and we might get a glimpse of her at the foot of the cross on Good Friday. You really couldn't mention her too frequently; it was a slippery slope to idolatry.

Like the unspoken polarizations of the Baptists and Catholics in Knoxville, Tennessee, the church in general has had similar internal wrangling over the identity of Mary throughout its history.

Religious art often portrays her as a pale, humble figure whose body is shrouded in robes – usually blue – with her eyes lowered submissively and hands folded. But these desexualized images of Mary are relatively late interpretations, from the late Renaissance into the nineteenth century.

Earlier images are more human, emotive, and realistic. During the Middle Ages, for example, artists depicted Mary nursing her baby with bared breasts, playing with a toddler Jesus, and fully alive. We see her, too, mourning at the death of Jesus, suffering as he suffered and vigilant at the foot of the cross.

Although the meek and mild Mary is only one depiction of many, it may be the most familiar. But the Catholic Church calls on Mary as a source of strength and protection.

The familiar incantation of the Rosary invokes Mary's present strength and shelter.

> Hail Mary, full of grace, the Lord is with you.
> Blessed are you among women and blessed is the fruit of your womb, Jesus.
> Holy Mary, Mother of God, pray for us sinners, now and at the hour of our death.

Many call on her as the Mother of us all, who protects and loves – Mary of constant mercy.

As we hear this classic Advent passage again, we remember the context of Mary's song. She has just told her troubling secret to her cousin Elisabeth: she is pregnant. I can imagine that she just blurted it out, telling the surreal tale of the angelic visit and the pronouncement that Mary's own child would be God's Prince of Peace and the Good News to God's people. What should she make of it all – this young teenage girl?

And then, Mary sings! We hear her song, the Magnificat, during this Advent season – to the soaring music of Vivaldi, Mozart, Berlioz or Bach.

As we might imagine, Mary's song voices gratitude and wonder, humility and hope. And, frequently, that's all we hear. But, if we are to kindle the fire of Advent in a way that's faithful to the Magnificat, we must listen further to this surprising, shocking poem.

Sister Miriam Therese Winter's hymn-like setting paraphrases the scriptural text and joins it with a beautiful plaintive melody:

My soul gives glory to my God;
My heart pours out its praise.
God lifted up my lowliness
In many marvelous ways.

The theme is clear: that which is lowly is lifted up, and that which assumes entitlement to superior place is humbled. And it's God who does this political action.

This is a theme throughout the scriptures. Politics and prayer, protest and song are intrinsically joined, part of the same holy task of setting the world right.

I had an opportunity for several years to teach a class on the role of music in social change movements at a university in the Pacific Northwest. In preparing the curriculum, I learned that music was instrumental (pun fully intended) in every protest movement in the United States and in other countries as well. One of the most powerful traditions of musical protest was that of the labor movement, accompanying the struggles of miners and factory workers and field laborers to gain for themselves healthy working conditions, a livable wage, and reasonable working hours. The music was the soul of the movement, and it fueled the engine of change for millions who were suffering.

Pete Seeger sang:

Come all of you good workers, good news to you I'll tell
Of how that good old union has come in here to dwell.
Which side are you on? Which side are you on?
Don't scab for the bosses; don't listen to their lies.
Us poor folks haven't got a chance unless we organize. (Reese)

I see Mary's Magnificat as a labor protest song, an uprising of the poor who are the economic captives of the rich. In economic uprisings in Latin America, her song has been widely used to empower poor people. She has been a spiritually present advocate of the poor and her voice is strong and uncompromised in its insistence that God is on the side of the lowly and struggling.

Mary sings of her son, God's anointed one, who will turn the economic tables, set the power structures right, bring autonomy to human relationships.

The message is clear: God's priority is to right the wrongs that have prevailed because some people and governments have promoted the agenda of the rich and powerful to the horrific detriment of poor folks. This is antithetical to the way of God, and always has been. Centuries before, Miriam and Hannah sang the same proclamation, and now Mary announces that God's Promised One will turn the world right.

Mary's Magnificat puts the power of Christ, the claim that God is on their side, into the voices and lives of those who are held down because they are without political and economic power. Mary is the friend and champion of those who struggle.

Theologian Dorothee Soelle notes that until the Middle Ages:

> Mary was not a particularly popular figure in the liturgy… or in literature under the influence of the clergy. [Rather], she belonged to the poor, the unlettered, the mendicant friars, the people. She was known as the "Madonna of rogues"… the Madonna of the impoverished rural [class], who could not help being at odds with the… stringent laws that defined and protected property. (Soelle, *Strength of the Weak,* 45)

A number of years ago, "base communities" formed among Catholics in Central and South America. These communities of faith were made up of poor, working men and women and their priests. Together, they studied the scriptures and discussed how the Bible's stories of liberation applied to their personal, social, and political lives – how they could make a difference in the world and stop suffering. A priest compiled a book that captured a conversation on the Magnificat.

Here's part of that conversation:

> The priest read: "God has scattered the proud in the imaginations of their hearts, put the mighty down from their thrones, and exalted those of low degree; has filled the hungry with good things, and the rich has sent empty away."
>
> The people responded: "Bravo! But, Father, that doesn't sound like the Mary we hear about in the cathedral…"
>
> The priest asked them to explain. They pulled out a picture. "Here she is. She is standing on a crescent moon and is wearing a crown. She has rings on her fingers. She has a blue robe embroidered with gold.'"
>
> "That does sound like a different Mary from the Mary of the song," the priest agreed. "Do you think the picture has betrayed the Mary of the song?"
>
> They thought and concluded: "The Mary who said that God 'has exalted those of low degree' would not have left all of her

OUT ON A LIMB

friends so she could stand on the moon. Take her off the moon!

"The Mary who said that God 'has put down the mighty from their thrones' would not be wearing a crown. Take off her crown!

"The Mary who said that God 'has sent the rich empty away' would not be wearing rings on her fingers. Take off her rings!

"The Mary who said that God has 'filled the hungry with good things' would not have left people who were still hungry, to wear a silk robe. Take off her robe!"

And then, with anguish, they saw what they had done. "But Father, this is not right! We're — we're doing a striptease of the Virgin."

"Very well," said the priest. "If you don't like the way Mary looks in this picture, what do you think the Mary of the song would look like?"

"The Mary of the song would not be standing on the moon. She would be standing in the dirt and dust where we stand. She would have on an old hat like the rest of us, to keep the sun from causing her to faint. She would have rough hands like ours and old clothes like the rest of us." (R. McA. Brown, 85-88)

Do you see her? Can you hear her teaching Jesus and hear those same messages spoken years later in his own voice?

That Mary – the one who sings from the pages of Luke's gospel – knew that God favored her, lifted her. She had a message to bring to the world: that God's desire was for human beings to live rightly and to distribute the resources of God's good creation with kindness and equity.

What fire did Mary kindle as she awaited the arrival of Jesus? Of course, like any young woman expecting her first child, the fires of motherhood and attachment burned in her body and spirit. She continued to ponder the angel's visit and the meaning of the vision. Perhaps she rubbed her belly with wonder and just a bit of fear as she contemplated the future.

As Mary waited, that song continued to sing in her soul; it kindled the fires of revolution, of justice and of God's order of things. All this she would pass on to the one who would give his life for this poetic seed of the Realm of God.

Might we, too, kindle the fire of love and mercy, the fire of economic justice, in order to prepare the way of the Lord?

Many of us have spent passion, time and energy working for justice; I know that's true. But what about the sort of imbalance of economic power of which Mary sings? The United States and other Western nations are divided into the haves and have-nots. And we know that our nation often subscribes to an ethic that demands that we pull ourselves up by our own bootstraps; if you work hard, you'll get ahead. If you don't have in abundance, you must not have the right work ethic.

However, a growing number of us see the fallacy of these adages. We know that people suffer. We know that the rich get richer. We know that the poor are punished with higher interest rates and even higher fuel prices.

Several years ago, plastic bracelets inscribed with the letters WWJD were popular in evangelical circles. The idea was to ask, "What would Jesus do?" when one found oneself in a moral dilemma. Perhaps we could change the question and ask, "What would Mary do?" What would Mary do to pave the way for God's ways to be born among us? Perhaps we could start a new trend: WWMD? Only the bold and tenacious would wear the bracelets.

In the Middle Ages, the common people would cheer loudly when the Magnificat was read. The hierarchy couldn't stop it, but attempted to limit it by decreeing that they could only cheer three times. The song is dangerous; it stirs a passion for equity.

In Guatemala in the 1980s the government banned the reading and singing of the Magnificat; they didn't want this powerful, spirit-filled poem to fuel the revolutionary spirit of the people. It was considered so subversive that they were afraid it would incite the oppressed people to riot.

This song and others like it have been sung by God's prophets and visionaries for ages. Songs of joy and gratitude, of justice and revolution, of hope and risk.

How can we sing this song of fire and justice and not be moved to action in our world? Can Mary's song inspire us to take to the streets to challenge what's not right in our city and our nation? Will its radical message stir the same spirit in us?

If we hear her song, we must respond by lifting up those who are on the bottom rung! And if we're on the higher rungs, we can step down and give our place away. We can work to make things a little more equal, give something up for the good of another. We can use less – and pass on what we don't use.

We can tell what we know about God's politic, to public officials, to friends and neighbors. Don't let Jesus – or Mary – be misrepresented.

And if you're struggling, if you feel like you're one of the last and least, know you have a friend in Mary – and in Jesus – and in all those who seek to follow them. You can take the power like Mary does, with gratitude, wonder, fire and revolution.

You see, Mary isn't either the bold revolutionary or the demure, silent mother. She's both. She's a human being who lives and sings the love and passion of God, and prepares the way for God to bring hope to the world – in Jesus and in herself.

Mary paints a portrait of the One for whom we prepare. If we will sing her song – with our voices and our lives – then perhaps, here and now, this Christ will come again.

2

KINDLE THE FIRE

Isaiah 2:1-5

The vision that Isaiah saw concerning Judah and Jerusalem:

In days to come, the mountain of Yahweh's house shall be established as the highest of the mountains, and shall be raised above the hills; all the nations shall stream to it. Many peoples shall come and say, "Come, let us go up to the mountain of Yahweh, to the house of the God of Jacob; that we may learn the way." For out of Zion shall go forth instruction, and the word of God from Jerusalem.

The Holy One shall judge between the nations, and shall arbitrate for many peoples; they shall beat their swords into ploughshares, and their spears into pruning hooks; nation shall not lift up sword against nation, neither shall they learn war any more. O house of Jacob, come, let us walk in the light of the Lord!

Romans 13:11-14

Besides this, you know what time it is; now is the moment for you to awaken from sleep. For salvation is nearer to us now than when we came to believe; the night is far gone, the day is near. Let us then lay aside all that is destructive and put on the garment of light; let us live honorably as in the day, not in reveling and drunkenness, not in debauchery and licentiousness, not in quarreling and jealousy. Instead, put on Christ.

છ

ADVENT IS A TIME of watchfulness and waiting, not just the church's countdown to Christmas.

Advent's purpose is to offer us the opportunity to prepare ourselves and the church for the coming of Christ: to be spiritually awake enough to recognize the appearance of God-with-us, Emmanuel. During Advent, we live in hopeful expectation that, even though the times may be dark in the world and in our own souls, daybreak is close at hand.

Advent begins in our darkest time of year in the northern hemisphere – symbolic of our greatest existential despair. It leads us expectantly toward what we consider to be the ultimate manifestation of peace and love, the birth of Christ.

Advent is a season of hope and promise rather than one of fulfillment. Advent proclaims that we cannot truly experience the hope, peace, love and joy of Christmas if we have not traveled into the depths of our own hearts. Advent calls us to expect, prepare and wait for the inbreaking of this God of peace into the shadows of a broken world and into our deep fear, skewed priorities, and anxieties.

Waiting is something that many of us don't do so well. It's a skill that our culture just doesn't nurture. We live in an instant world. We turn electrical appliances on and expect them to produce immediate results. We order food and it appears without our ploughing and planting. The internet can answer almost any question that we can think of and millions that we've never considered. Can you imagine writing a letter about an urgent matter and then actually waiting for a reply by post?

We kindle our Advent fire of expectation – of vigil. We settle in to watch and wait.

And then, as we're about to nod off around the warm winter fire, we hear that cry from the Apostle Paul:

You know what time it is; now is the moment for you to awaken from sleep. For salvation is nearer to us now than when we came to believe; the night is far gone, the day is near. (Romans 13:11-12)

This is the message that always begins our Advent worship: Wake up! Watch. Pay attention! Open your eyes to the signs of the wonder and work of God. See the change and power coming into the world! Sometimes this change is seen as doom, trouble, upheaval or reordering of life.

During Advent, we hear those words from the prophet Isaiah, made familiar to us from the music of Handel's Messiah, those words that give us a vision of a world made right by God's entry into it:

They shall beat their swords into ploughshares, and their spears into pruning hooks; nation shall not lift up sword against nation, neither shall they learn war any more. O house of Jacob, come, let us walk in the light of God! (Isaiah 2:5)

Isaiah offers us something worth waiting for: the power, beauty, order and love of God coming into a broken and struggling world. It is this for which we wait, this that we position ourselves to receive.

Keep awake, the text says. Keep the hope alive. Live in the presence of God – in peace and expectation. To keep awake is to be deeply attentive to God's effort to break into our stress and anxiety, sitting vigil with the world in the way a compassionate friend refuses to leave the side of someone in need.

Watch and wait. God is coming into the world.

What could this message possibly have to say to us today? Do these promises of peace and assurances of things made right have any relevance to our world? Does God still offer hope in the face of the desperate warring and struggles of both politics and our psyches?

What are we waiting for when we sit at this vigil fire? Have we slipped into hopelessness and resignation? Do we just accept it as the way of the world that increasing numbers of people live in economic despair? That our personal agency is at stake? Or do we have hope that God can make a way?

We kindle the fire of hope. And we wait, Oh God, for signs of your coming!

Over a hundred million people around the world currently experience depression, including fifteen percent of older Americans and ten percent of American teenagers. And our nation was alarmed by the multiple bullying-related suicides of gay teenagers in late 2010 and early 2011. (*Sources:* Healthline, Geriatric Mental Health Foundation, National Institute of Mental Health, Stokell)

We kindle the fire of hope. And we wait, Oh God, for signs of your coming!

War and violence, rage and revenge cause our world to live in fear. Seemingly random terrorist attacks, aggressive actions of nation against nation.

We kindle the fire of hope. And we wait, Oh God, for signs of your coming!

Our own lives, too, long for love and for peace. We know our own struggles and we hear each other's.

We kindle the fire of hope. And we wait, Oh God, for signs of your coming!

The apostle Paul writes in the epistle to the Romans:

> Let us then lay aside all that is destructive and put on the garment of light; let us live honorably as in the day, not in reveling and drunkenness, not in debauchery and licentiousness, not in quarreling and jealousy. Instead, put on Christ. (Romans 13:13-14)

Clear away the things that distract you from watching for Christ. Face in God's direction. You may just catch a glimpse of the one who can turn it all around. Live in that direction so that you'll be ready to grasp Christ's way.

As we've experienced for over a decade, the first Sunday of Advent coincides with the marking of World AIDS Day. Through the years, we could easily say that we've waited and watched for things to change – for better prevention, for a cure. But these words from Paul's letter to the church at Rome encourage us to live-as-if, to prepare ourselves for our hope by getting ready.

A beautiful example of this sort of Advent preparation happened among us – here in this church. Patsy, an active member of the church, was in her forties. She'd been an intravenous drug user and had contracted HIV. This was, of course, in the time before anti-retroviral medications.

Patsy loved life – her family, her partner, her church, and God. She used her imagination to see what God would have her do. She would turn once more from the brink of death because of some vision of God's next project for her to pursue to bring hope and life as she waited: plant a garden to feed those with AIDS, begin a group to talk about having hope, speak with news reporters to point out that even women get sick.

Patsy lived when she should have died. And many others did, too, because she dared to wake up when the night seemed to overtake. She kindled the fires of hope and waited by living as Christ in this community.

The gospel writers remind us to keep awake, for you do not know on what day God's anointed one is coming.

Well, we may not be good at waiting or not knowing when the thing we're awaiting will come. But we spend much time doing just that.

Waiting is just a part of life, and creative waiting – waiting during which God forms us and prepares us for what is to come – seems to be how God works in us. When we're in life's waiting places, we get still and receptive. We reflect and see more clearly.

During Advent's waiting, we consider what it means for Christ to come into the world, for Jesus to enter our own lives. We examine our priorities, our ways of life, and perhaps we realize that we can be Christ's presence in the world, another incarnation.

We need Advent to make ourselves ready, for the waiting place can change us, open us.

We kindle the fire of hope because the God who was present in the birth of Jesus promises to be born again and again and again. This waiting is infused with anticipation.

Can you imagine that God will break into our world, into your world?

Perhaps if we kindle the fire, this fire in our sanctuary and the fire in our own hearts, and wait, if we watch expectantly for what God will do, just perhaps, God-with-us will be born again.

Perhaps, in the places of great need in our lives and in our world; perhaps, in those given-up places, those situations of resignation, we'll see the light appear. Will you kindle the fire of hope and expectation, of renewal and imagination, and wait?

EPIPHANY

3

BY ANOTHER ROAD

Matthew 2:1-12

In the time of King Herod, after Jesus was born in Bethlehem of Judea, wise men from the East came to Jerusalem, asking, "Where is the child? For we observed his star at its rising, and have come to pay him homage." When King Herod heard this, he was frightened, and all Jerusalem with him; and calling together all the chief priests and scribes of the people, he inquired of them where the Messiah was to be born. They told him, "In Bethlehem of Judea; for so it has been written by the prophet: 'And you, Bethlehem, in the land of Judah, are by no means least among the rulers of Judah; for from you shall come a ruler who is to shepherd my people Israel.'"

Then Herod secretly called for the wise men and learned from them the exact time when the star had appeared. Then he sent them to Bethlehem, saying, "Go and search diligently for the child; and when you have found him, bring me word so that I may also go and pay him homage." When they had heard the king, they set out; and there, ahead of them, went the star that they had seen at its rising, until it stopped over the place where the child was. When they saw that the star had stopped, they were overwhelmed with joy. On entering the house, they saw the child with Mary his mother; and they knelt down and paid him homage. Then, opening their treasure-chests, they offered him gifts of gold, frankincense, and myrrh. And having been warned in a dream not to return to Herod, they left for their own country by another road.

૯૭

AT THE TURNING of this New Year, we may be ready to take stock, to reflect and question. We may revisit decisions and priorities, review choices and actions. We think of a new calendar year as a new beginning, a chance to implement intentional change.

And yet, we resist, jaded as we are from failed attempts, or hesitant as we are to implement change at all. We find it challenging to envision – much less live – our lives on a different road.

Today, we celebrate the feast of the Epiphany. Epiphany, of course, means revelation or manifestation, and the primary images of Epiphany are the star that appears and leads the way to the infant Jesus, and the Magi, those visitors from foreign lands who followed the star.

Themes of Epiphany include Journey, Signs, Surprises, Fears, Insights, Discoveries, Change. Epiphany offers us rich, appropriate themes for both the beginning of a New Year and for the season of winter.

The Magi were "from the east", Persia, perhaps. They were clearly not Jews. Rather, they would have been considered Gentiles, pagans; they were outside the chosen people, not those for whom the star shone.

Some theorize that the Magi may have been priests of the Zoroastrian religion, in which fire represents God's light and wisdom or the illuminated mind. They were astrologers, and reading stars for signs of God's activity was their tradition, their religion. R.T. France, in his commentary on Matthew's gospel, says that the *magos* (the Greek word) were educated men who advised kings. The title usually referred to magicians, astrologers, or interpreters of dreams. (France, 66)

In the first century, astrologers believed that stars heralded the birth of human beings who were destined for greatness.

Now, the Magi may have been actual people, or they may

represent, in a Jungian sense, those of any tradition who seek with courage, those who are willing – for the sake of truth and hope – to follow the light, to explore any course, to find the places where God breaks into human life.

Either way, we can find profound meaning in this tale and an invitation for this New Year.

The Magi explored, geographically and spiritually, in pursuit of this light. They noticed, as astrologers, that something was changing. And they set off in hot pursuit. They interpreted the changes in the heavens – as they would – as a sign that God was up to something.

The star led them to a foreign place, a foreign religion, and their route was constantly uncertain and shifting. They sought first within their own tradition, as they studied the heavens. As they followed the sign, they entered the symbolic world of the Hebrew prophets and the religious life of the Jews. There's fear around such crossings: fear of deception, or fear of deeper truth. Or fear of ambiguity. But the Magi were on a quest, and that led them to observe another faith through the practice of their own.

Now, we imagine – through years of nativity pageants and model crèches – that the Magi headed straight for the stable. But, did you notice? The Magi followed the star, not to Bethlehem, but to Jerusalem! There the scribes and Pharisees disclosed to them what the scriptures say about the Messiah. They learned the expectation of the Jewish tradition through the writings of the prophets.

Then Herod, the Roman-appointed Gentile king of Israel, sent them to find the child. Herod was afraid when he heard the message of the Magi. He was the king and was threatened by anything he couldn't control, especially the prophecy of a replacement king. Herod's state was one of fear, of anxiety, of the need to control.

We know the signs – how it is to live in fear rather than in love, when we allow our fears to dominate us and keep us from living freely.

So, in his panic, Herod called the religious authorities to discern the seriousness of the threat. Then he acted in secrecy and deception. He directed the Magi:

> Go and search diligently for the child; and when you have found him, bring me word so that I may also go and pay him homage. (Matthew 2:8)

Did you notice that Herod never looked for the star himself? He didn't seek, didn't risk probing the possibilities or opening himself to the experience of something powerful that was occurring.

The contrast is stunning! The Magi were open, seeking, trusting, searching for wisdom – regardless of the source – and spiritually curious. They were looking for something beyond themselves, moving with a sense of wonder.

They let their search guide them as they changed course in their pursuit of God's new way. They headed to Jerusalem – and now they were sent to Bethlehem by a new story, a new signpost along the way. They learned; deliberated; decided. Even though they were directed by Herod, the sure guidance of the star resumed.

Sometimes that which guides our journey fades, shines too dimly to lead. Perhaps we lose our way in pursuing God and wisdom for living. But the journey of the Magi tells us that when one source of revelation ends, other possibilities for wisdom and truth can guide us.

The Magi found their way – with the signs in the stars, with the Jewish promise, and with their own cosmic revelation. They were motivated by both head and heart. They sought and found. They expressed wonder and deep joy.

And then, yet again, the Spirit changed their course. They went home by a different route. And they surely went home as different people. They had been formed and changed as their spiritual curiosity led them to the birth of one who would include others like them and teach about a God who invited their sort of seeking.

In this New Year, what changes of course might you take? Are there other roads that call you? Can you trust the guidance that your life brings to lead you with purpose and love?

Like the poet Robert Frost, we may see the roads diverge before us. The differences are subtle, though plain. We can choose – or not. We can decide – resolve – today that the year ahead holds revelations and opportunities to seek and find.

The Magi followed the light, even when it led them to unimagined places and strange traditions, when it took them before mad, unscrupulous dictators and on dangerous, unknown, unplanned routes. They followed the Light, the Wisdom, the Star. They chose the road less traveled by – in search of the Way of hope, of love and wonder.

Are we willing – or even eager – to join the Magi's caravan, to head home by a different road, to take the road less traveled, to seek wisdom, to change our course, take a different way?

I hope that we are and that we will, even in small and simple ways. I hope that we will look into the night sky of our lives and find the light that beckons us and that we'll follow it with courage.

Perhaps these words from the poet Robert Frost can become ours:

I shall be telling this with a sigh
Somewhere ages and ages hence:
Two roads diverged in a wood, and I –
I took the one less traveled by,
And that has made all the difference. (Frost, 9)

4

IN DEEP WATER

Isaiah 43:1-3

But now thus says the Lord, he who created you, O Jacob, he who formed you, O Israel: Do not fear, for I have redeemed you; I have called you by name, you are mine. When you pass through the waters, I will be with you; and through the rivers, they shall not overwhelm you; when you walk through fire you shall not be burned, and the flame shall not consume you. For I am the Lord your God, the Holy One of Israel, your Savior.

Luke 3:15-22

As the people were filled with expectation, and all were questioning in their hearts concerning John, whether he might be the Messiah, John answered all of them by saying, "I baptize you with water; but one who is more powerful than I is coming; I am not worthy to untie the thong of his sandals. He will baptize you with the Holy Spirit and fire. His winnowing fork is in his hand, to clear his threshing floor and to gather the wheat into his granary; but the chaff he will burn with unquenchable fire." So, with many other exhortations, he proclaimed the good news to the people.

But Herod the ruler, who had been rebuked by him because of Herodias, his brother's wife, and because of all the evil things that Herod had done, added to them all by shutting up John in prison.

Now when all the people were baptized, and when Jesus also had been baptized and was praying, the heaven was opened, and the Holy Spirit descended upon him in bodily form like a dove. And a voice came from heaven, "You are my Son, the Beloved; with you I am well pleased."

ℰℐ

WELL… WE'RE BACK to John the Baptist again! We caught a glimpse of him and his wild preaching during Advent, as he called people to repentance to prepare for the coming of the Christ.

Years later, many years later, he's still at it: preaching and baptizing. I guess some things never change.

I love the baptism scene in the film, *O Brother, Where Art Thou?* (Coen). We see those country folk coming from every direction, dressed in white, processing with focus and attention as they make their way to the muddy river. The rogue main characters watch in rapt amazement and bewilderment. They feel the power, the mystery, as vows are being spoken, and as, one by one, grateful men and women are plunged into the river.

From this scene in the film, baptisms we've witnessed, or the story of John the Baptist in the gospels, we know that something important "happens" when one is baptized, something that is mysterious and powerful, traditional and yet subversive.

But what does it all really mean? What is this thing that John the Baptist and Jesus did, which became so central to the Christian experience that much of the Christian world now calls it a sacrament – that is, a special experience of the Holy?

Did John make this up? Why is it important? Does it actually *do* something? Is it just an act of initiation – or does it have deeper significance?

The symbology of baptism is, of course, washing and preparation, and yet it is a convergence of inner and outer meanings, as is most ritual: a purification of body and soul.

We know that baptism rituals pre-date Jesus and John, pre-date Christianity itself. With the discovery of the Dead Sea scrolls, we know that the Qumran community, a religious group centered about twenty-five miles south of Jerusalem, practiced a ritual of daily baptism for cleansing their bodies and their spirits. Some scholars speculate that John the Baptist may have been associated with the community at Qumran and encouraged that spiritual practice beyond the sect.

I believe that the act of baptism touches something deep in our souls. Baptism – washing – speaks of the need of all humankind for cleansing, new birth, a new and clean beginning, or the marking of a point of profound spiritual change.

In baptism we're marked, washed, identified with all others who have received this mark. Baptism is anointing – preparation for life to come; this was true for Jesus and is significant for all who come to the font. We receive this washing, this anointing, marking and naming as we begin our faith life, and – often – as we renew it.

Consider the element itself. The substance and the metaphor of water have played a part in the story of our faith – in the Jewish and Christian scriptures. And water is the Source of life, really – a constant, primal need. It is necessary for growth, filled with nutrients. Water enables life to flourish, to bloom, to emerge with beauty. It sustains health and keeps our bodies cool. Water comprises seventy-five percent of our bodies – one hundred and five pounds of water is standing before you. Please don't do the math.

And the baptismal prayer, the blessing of water, reminds us of water images in the story of our faith:

> Eternal God, when nothing existed but chaos,
>   you swept across the dark waters and brought forth light.

> In the days of Noah you saved those on the ark through water.
> After the flood you set a rainbow in the clouds.
> When you saw your people as slaves in Egypt,
>   you led them to freedom through the sea.

Their children you brought through the Jordan
to the land which you promised.

In the fullness of time you sent Jesus, nurtured in the water of
[Mary's] womb.

He was baptized by John and anointed by your Spirit. He
called his disciples to share in the baptism of death and
resurrection and to make disciples of all nations.

Pour out your Holy Spirit to bless this gift of water and all who
receive it, to cleanse us from all that marks us as other than
beloved, to clothe us in garments of righteousness, to name
us as your people – holy and blessed, to give us an outward
sign of the inner reality that we are your people and you are
our God – our wisdom, our strength, our joy.
(*United Methodist Book of Worship*, 90)

The images are rich, inviting deep reflection. They offer meaning
for us in this ancient rite that is still a part of our tradition.

We reflect today on the baptism of Jesus – we heard the brief
story. But, you might think, if baptism is about cleansing and repentance, about renewal and being marked as God's own, why
should Jesus not stand on the bank and watch the others or invite
them to come to him for baptism: those who need a second chance,
those who have waded out deep into trouble? Let the people who
have drifted so far that nobody can help them, let them come.

But, you see, baptism is also about remembering, remembering
who we are and the connection with God that sustains us. Our
Isaiah passage recalls the promise of the presence of God, invoking
the image of going through the deep waters of life. Baptism is being
immersed in the power of God's love and remembering that we are
drenched in God's presence, especially when life is tough. I need
that – and I suspect you do, too, as we navigate life's challenges.

Did you notice that John the Baptist goes through those deep, challenging waters? I had not paid much attention to this part of the passage before. But – right in the middle of this reading, John the Baptist is imprisoned by Herod, even as he's baptizing, including baptizing Jesus! Baptism happens right in the middle of life! This event emphasizes that baptism isn't a matter of spirit only, but a matter of body and politics and social challenge.

Though the forms of baptism vary, the symbols are rich and allow us to feel the touch of God. Baptism by immersion symbolizes dying to the old life and rising to new life in Christ. Baptism by pouring or sprinkling evokes images of the pouring out of God's spirit. In baptism we are named, initiated, chosen, washed, marked, gifted, anointed and sent forth. We are identified as one of God's own. We bear in our bodies the mark of promise.

Several years ago, a woman called Rebecca told me about her baptism. She was about twelve years old and had experienced the love of Jesus in her life. She approached her pastor about being baptized and a date was set.

But just before he baptized her, the pastor – who had evidently decided that Rebecca was gay, although she herself didn't know it then – told Rebecca that he knew what kind of person she was and that her baptism was a mistake. So, while he did actually baptize her, it was a shameful and sad experience for Rebecca.

We baptized Rebecca again. And we all knew that baptism was about acceptance, about the love of God awakened, about God's mark on Rebecca's life – through it all.

This promise of God-with-us is given to us by water and the spirit – on our foreheads, in our hearts, in our living. Even when we feel like life is overwhelming, when the floods of doubt, frustration, pain, depression, and loneliness threaten to drown us – to bury us alive – we can feel again the waters of baptism and know that we are immersed in the love and care of God.

We sometimes need to return to the waters of baptism to come home, to start anew, to realize that the spirit of God is poured out on us still, to be cleansed again and rise to newness of life, to receive the outpouring of the spirit.

At the Mother of Peace Orphanage in Mutoko, Zimbabwe, the children are not required to attend worship – but almost all of them do. The children, most of them under twelve and many under six, are summoned to services by the clanging of a cow bell. They run, often playing and singing as they approach the chapel. And then something changes.

As they slow down and walk into the sanctuary, each child stops just inside the doors, dips small fingers into the water of the baptismal font and marks their forehead with their wet fingers. Then, with focused, serious faces, they kneel on the floor and begin to pray aloud, simultaneously but curiously alone. Something changed when they took that water for themselves.

Do you need to touch that water this morning, to hear the water's vitality and experience its washing? To witness its touch in the lives of others, to know its promise of life and belonging?

As we remember the baptism of Jesus, remember your own baptism. Experience the connection we have with the people of God – the baptized – particularly in this place.

As you come for communion, I invite you to come to the font, reach into the waters of baptism once again and remember. As you touch the water, you may touch your forehead and know that you are once again and forever marked as God's Beloved.

5

MARRIED TO GOD

Isaiah 62:1-5

For Zion's sake I will not keep silent, and for Jerusalem's sake I will not rest, until her vindication shines out like the dawn, and her salvation like a burning torch. The nations shall see your vindication, and all the kings your glory; and you shall be called by a new name that the mouth of the Lord will give. You shall be a crown of beauty in the hand of the Lord, and a royal diadem in the hand of your God. You shall no more be termed Forsaken, and your land shall no more be termed Desolate; but you shall be called My Delight Is in Her, and your land Married; for the Lord delights in you, and your land shall be married. For as a young man marries a young woman, so shall your builder marry you, and as the bridegroom rejoices over the bride, so shall your God rejoice over you.

John 2:1-11

On the third day there was a wedding in Cana of Galilee, and the mother of Jesus was there. Jesus and his disciples had also been invited to the wedding. When the wine gave out, the mother of Jesus said to him, "They have no wine." And Jesus said to her, "Woman, what concern is that to you and to me? My hour has not yet come." His mother said to the servants, "Do whatever he tells you." Now standing there were six stone water jars for the Jewish rites of purification, each holding twenty or thirty gallons. Jesus said to them, "Fill the jars with water." And they filled them up to the brim. He said to them, "Now draw some out, and take it to the chief steward." So they took it. When the steward tasted the water that had become wine, and did not know where it came from (though the servants who had drawn the water knew), the steward called the bridegroom and said to him, "Everyone serves the good wine first, and then the inferior wine after the guests have become drunk. But you have kept the good wine until now." Jesus did this, the first of his signs, in Cana of Galilee, and revealed his glory; and his disciples believed in him.

∾

BOTH OUR HEBREW text and our gospel lesson use the images of marriage and weddings.

Now marriage isn't exactly a theme of the scriptures! The Bible doesn't have very much to say about marriage – even less than we might think. Take Adam and Eve, for example. Some see them as the first "married couple". Really now? No marriage promises there.

Many of us know the marriage vows from the pages of scripture, those beautiful words spoken by Ruth to Naomi:

> Entreat me not to leave you or to return from following you,
> For where you go, I will go. Where you lodge, I will lodge.
> Your people will be my people and your God my God.
> (Ruth 1:16-17)

The image of marriage is used to describe relationship with God. The lavish poetry of the Song of Songs speaks of love, desire, and marriage. And the writer of the book of Revelation refers repeatedly to the people of God as the bride of Christ and their union as the marriage feast of the Lamb.

These images paint a vivid portrait of the nature of God's steadfast love and passion for us – and of God's faithfulness to creation. They reveal how God binds God's self to us, looking beyond our shortcomings, clinging to us as a lover does, seeing our value and beauty.

Perhaps more than any other characteristic, marriage means

intimacy, knowing and being known. The Source of Life and Love wants to be in intimate relationship with us.

At the outset of Jesus' ministry, we find him at a wedding, turning water into wine. The water of purification becomes the wine of jubilation. An embarrassing shortage is turned to an extravagant outpouring of celebration.

I wonder why this was Jesus' first sign. Perhaps Jesus points to another marriage celebration? Is this a sign of God's extravagance as a wedding partner and the celebration of the union of God and God's people? The miracle suggests radical transformation from the old to the new, full of richness and joy.

Wine at a wedding feast offers the images of wine's richness of ferment; like love, it takes time to ripen into the stuff of conviviality and celebration, a toast to life, an extravagance – like passionate love.

Marriage has profound spiritual overtones: the joining of souls as one, becoming one flesh. Perhaps that's why some want it as their sole domain; it's a sacred commodity. Some want marriage as their own, to define it and own it and claim it, to decide who is afforded the right to marry. That's not such a foreign religious phenomenon, really; some want "salvation" as their own – to define it and own it and claim it, decide who can have it and who cannot.

The power of Isaiah's proclamation about God's love is stunning. After chapters of the prophet's proclamation of God's judgment on the exiled nation of Israel, this portion of the book of Isaiah proclaims a new day. All within two chapters, the prophet announces to God's people:

Arise, shine; for your light has come, and the glory of God has risen upon you! (Isaiah 60:1)

The spirit of the Lord God is upon me because the Lord has

anointed me; and has sent me to bring good news to the oppressed. (Luke 4:18)

And then a love poem, really, declares a new name for Israel:

You shall no more be termed Forsaken, and your land shall no more be termed Desolate; but you shall be called My Delight Is in Her. (Isaiah 62:4)

One translation says it like this:

You shall be called "My desire is in her," and your land, "married," for Adonai desires you. (*Complete Jewish Bible*, Isaiah 62:4)

The prophet continues…

For as a young man marries a young woman, so shall your builder marry you, and as the bridegroom rejoices over the bride, so shall your God rejoice over you. (Isaiah 62:5)

Do you hear what I hear? That God's desire is to *marry* God's people.

Priests and nuns have used that imagery for centuries. But have we ever dared envision it for ourselves? Married to God – what could that possibly mean?

First, it reimagines the nature of God and God's view of us. This is not the portrait of God, the judge. Nor is it the stern parent waiting for me to misbehave. Rather, the Holy One adores us, believes in us, nurtures and holds us, is passionately in love with us, and desires to join in life with us – in body, mind, and spirit.

And just as with water to wine, when God joins with us, our lives are transformed. Everything changes.

While I was pastor of a congregation in Portland, Oregon, we had a beautiful window of opportunity to bless and record the marriages of over three thousand gay and lesbian couples.

(The background to this is that Basic Rights Oregon [BRO] had challenged the application of Oregon's constitution that granted marriage rights to two consenting adults. Following extended conversations between BRO staff and Multnomah County commissioners, the county granted marriage licenses to same-sex couples for several weeks in March 2004, before they were halted by a challenge to the state constitution.) We recruited more than twenty clergy from several faiths and celebrated marriages for many who thought this would never be possible for them.

I recall vividly the ceremony that I officiated for John and Phil, two men in their seventies. The couple had been together for over forty years. They said that they were just getting married because they finally could; they said it wouldn't really change anything for them. They were matter-of-fact about it, just wanted to get on with it. They certainly didn't see anything romantic about it.

Well, by the time John had repeated one sentence of the vows, both he and Phil and the friends who were with them were sobbing. You see, something *did* change. There was a new dimension to their union. The look on their faces was pure radiance; they found new delight in each other.

That lovely little song from the musical *Cabaret* expresses it like this:

How the world can change, it can change like that
Due to one little word: "Married"
… For you wake one day, look around and say, "Somebody
wonderful married me." (Ebb)

Perhaps, in the spirit of Isaiah, we could add a stanza:

And the voice of God pledges love to us,
And says we're his Beloved!
Like a lover finds pleasure and delight

So Yahweh's heart desires us.
And the old despair that was often there
Suddenly ceases to be
For the Spirit takes us as her bride –
The God of the universe clings to me.

Perhaps you've had a relationship with God for a long time. Maybe you've known God as parent, as Savior. Perhaps the Spirit has been your guide or Jesus your brother.

Or maybe you've had something of a dysfunctional relationship with God in which you've felt shame or guilt or fear. God may have been your judge or a harsh parent.

Come into this new relationship. The old way ceases to be. All is new and life-giving.

Both John and Isaiah speak of a transformation.

"You will no longer be called —," proclaims the prophet. "You will have a new name: Beloved, Married, My-Delight-Is-In-You." In this holy wedding of God and humans, we are offered God's faithfulness and passion, God's steadfast love that will not let us go.

Married to God who believes in you, joins with you – for good. We are God's Beloved. God's Delight. Married.

May you know it is so.

6

THE CHANGER AND THE CHANGED

Jonah 3:1-5, 10

The word of God came to Jonah, saying, "Get up, go to Nineveh, that great city, and proclaim to it the message that I tell you." So Jonah set out and went to Nineveh, according to the word of God. Now Nineveh was an exceedingly large city, a three days' walk across. Jonah began to go into the city, going a day's walk. And he cried out, "Forty days more, and Nineveh shall be overthrown!" And the people of Nineveh believed God; they proclaimed a fast, and everyone, great and small, put on sackcloth. When God saw what they did, how they turned from their evil ways, God's perspective changed, and God decided that no calamity would come upon the people.

Mark 1:14-20

After John was arrested, Jesus came to Galilee, proclaiming the good news of God, and saying, "The time is fulfilled, and the kingdom of God has come near; repent, and believe in the good news." As Jesus passed along the Sea of Galilee, he saw Simon and his brother Andrew casting a net into the sea – for they were fishermen. And Jesus said to them, "Follow me and I will make you fish for people." And immediately they left their nets and followed him. As he went a little farther, he saw James son of Zebedee and his brother John, who were in their boat mending the nets. Immediately he called them; and they left their father Zebedee in the boat with the hired men, and followed him.

❦

In her song *Change*, singer Tracy Chapman asks:

How bad, how good, does it need to get?
How many losses, how much regret?
What chain reaction would cause an effect?
Makes you turn around… Makes you change?

I'm continually amazed at the vigor with which many of us resist change. Because we fear the changes that might ensue, we take extreme measures to maintain the status quo: we control or overorganize ourselves and others to keep things in immutable order; we keep secrets and don't communicate with even those closest to us for fear of losing or shaking things up way too much.

So, inertia rules our lives – unchanging states – in the form of habits that need to be broken, resignation to life as it is, even when it isn't what we want it to be. This immovability dictates our activities and our relationships – and our spiritual lives as a result. Regardless of how unfulfilled or dissatisfied we are, we settle into our known, seemingly safe realities rather than risking the unknown future that change surely brings.

Now, part of my astonishment at our contentment with the status quo is looking around at the substance of everything we know about God and creation. Think about it. All creation is ever-changing – with seasons, the process of aging, the passage of time, growth and maturation. We change spiritually, physically, emotionally, and intellectually; are changed by chemical and mechanical stimuli. We could conclude that God's creation itself is change, embodies change, is natural. It's how life becomes, how life evolves, how it's sustained.

Even though, in traditional doctrine, God has been called immutable – never-changing – I suspect that has to do with the constancy of God's love rather than a description of an unmoving, stagnant divine nature. The story of Jonah at Nineveh includes a clear statement about God's ability and even desire to change. It says that, owing to the prophet's persuasion and the repentance of the people and the resultant changes that they made, God's mind is changed.

And think about Jesus, whose first sign of divine power was an act of change, changing water into wine, changing something plain and ordinary into something extraordinary and full of celebration. Jesus is the one whose life includes events like transfiguration by the Light of God – and the supreme change from death to resurrected life.

At the Bible's close, the words of Revelation point to a time when the trumpet will sound and we will all be changed.

We Christians speak of conversion and repentance as part of God's ultimate salvation that we receive. Salvation is wholeness, the spiritual change that brings us to life.

Both our texts for today center around change. They speak of a particular sort of change – not change that just happens, but change that turns people toward God and God's ways of self-giving and wholeness, of truth-seeking and loving our neighbors as ourselves.

Evidently, the people of Nineveh had lost their way. We don't know the nature of their troubles, but it was serious. It was about to take their life. So, God sent the prophet Jonah to awaken the ungodly city of Nineveh, in hopes that they would change.

Now, our text for today – as we know – isn't the whole story about the changes that take place. After running away once and getting in really big trouble, Jonah did what God sent him to do, but not without attitude. Jonah, frankly, didn't want the Ninevites to repent. He wanted them to suffer the consequences of their behavior. Can you relate? When we look around at our world, do you see anyone whose repentance would upset you? There may be one or two people whose repentance might distress me in my most unholy moments. I want them to reap their just rewards rather than change. (Not really – but I can understand Jonah's feelings.)

Jonah was angry with God's change of heart – interestingly, because he *knew* the nature of God. He *knew* that God will always soften and change if people realize their own need to change.

The people of the city saw the error of their ways and immediately they donned sackcloth and ashes, and turned and changed how they lived – so that they *could* live.

In our gospel lesson, Jesus had just offered a message about repenting – that is, turning. And then, two at a time, he called those who would become his followers to make a turn in their lives.

"Follow me," he invited them. "Leave your fishing life and join me. Help me fish for people; join me in offering the possibility of change, of newness of life, to others."

Jesus invited them to change their lives, stirred them up so that they, too, could move beyond business as usual, so that they, too, could bring justice, hope, and healing to others, and invite people to live authentically and honestly. The Changer and the changed – going on to become changers themselves.

Apparently, Simon and Andrew bit hook, line, and sinker. They immediately left their nets and followed Jesus. Interestingly, no words were exchanged, not a question was asked. What in the world just happened? After all, they depended on their work for their livelihood. They were to follow in their father's profession and sustain their community. These men had lives – families, communities, obligations. This is an astounding result. Immediately they changed their lives and left it all behind to follow Jesus. Jesus encountered them with such compelling love and power that they responded immediately.

Jesus' call to turn from ways that keep us from fullness of life is indeed – was then and is now – a call to change. It's a compelling call – because we recognize, if we're honest, that we want what Jesus has. We want peace and purpose. We long for the power to speak the truth. We want the compassion to give of ourselves. Deep down, we want to be all that we can be, despite the obstacles, despite the fear of change that keeps us from responding. We want what Jesus has.

If we answer Jesus' call to turn – to follow – we participate with God in change that needs to be made in our lives; we open ourselves to that unpredictable flow of the Spirit. We give ourselves to the processes of becoming all that we're created to be.

Perhaps you're going through the motions without joy, passion, direction. Or maybe your life is overly self-focused without time or thought for others. Perhaps you're living without luster, without wonder in your life – or even giving yourself to destructive habits.

If you feel out of alignment with what is ultimately important, if you feel disconnected from God or others, Jesus' call to turn and follow could bring some relief, could shape us all into our better selves and bring us more abundant life.

Jesus called these fishermen to change, but in order to realize their potential, to be those who healed and taught, they had to leave their nets behind so that they could take up what was new.

Perhaps we do, too.

We may need to leave our nets of dusty old faith that we haven't examined in years. We may have to leave our nets of non-action spirituality that's content with sitting. We may need to leave our nets of fear or selfishness. The nets of gossip and negativity and self-loathing must be left behind if we're going to have the kind of change that brings us life.

Jesus' call, you see, is for repentance – a call to turn completely around. We're traveling in one direction, and we're urged to make a full 180-degree turn in our hearts and spirits. Responding to Jesus' call to change has implications: for our relationships, for our politics, for how we use our resources.

At this intersection of our emotion, our willingness, our fear – when all of these things about ourselves come together and intersect with the call of Jesus, that's where the power lies. And that's where the meaning of this story lies for us today: at the intersection of our own emotional and spiritual state and the call of Jesus.

These are stories about something transformative coming into people's lives that calls them to change – but not into something or someone else. Rather, God's call is to be all that they – and we – are created to be.

Perhaps that's what we recognize in the stories of both Jonah and Jesus. Both stories tell of epiphanies – clear vision – of those who were missing something in their lives and needed to turn themselves around, so that they could have depth of life and joy and hope. Jesus called them to fish for people, called them, I think, to be what he was and to offer what he offered, and that is change that leads to depth of wellbeing, to newness of life, to purpose, and compassion.

What needs changing in your life? If you want to be all that you can be, if you want to live with compassion and kindness, if peace and joy seem somehow just out of reach, what needs to change?

If you want to live a more real and relevant spiritual life, if you want your life to make a positive difference to others in this world, if you're living with way too much stress or negativity, what needs to change?

Just recently, a friend of mine knew that she needed to make some changes in her life in order to be all that she could be. For many years, she had been silent and afraid. She had been discontent for way too long. She had lived to please her mother, all the while living a life full of secrets.

You see, my friend Natalie had come to realize that she was a transgender person. She longed to live truthfully and authentically, but fear kept her from facing and making this change that would help her be a whole person.

Natalie's father was a pastor – she was much like him and his pride and joy. After her father died, she became a pastor and kept his image alive for her mother, who invested time, money, and prayer in Natalie's ministry.

But finally, the need to make this change – to take up this new life – was so clear that she could no longer resist.

In her fear of disappointing her mother and with the terror of possible rejection pounding in her heart, she told her mother, who felt the predictable pain, fear, anger, and loss. She told Natalie that she needed time alone to just be with her news.

A month later, her mother was ready. She said that she had known something of the truth all along. Then, she said these grace-filled words: "You are mine. I love you, and, therefore, I want this change for you. I know it's who you are."

And then Natalie's mother asked something unbelievable: "Will you let me name you? If you had been a boy, your name would've been Nate. What do you think about that?"

And so it is with God, my friends, who meets us in our fear and in our need: ready to help us in our change, ready to give us a new name, and to bring us to our very best selves, to transform our fear with the love that promises to change everything.

7

BE THE VISION

Isaiah 58:6-8a, 11-12

Is not this the fast that I choose: to loose the bonds of injustice, to undo the thongs of the yoke, to let the oppressed go free, and to break every yoke?

Is it not to share your bread with the hungry, and bring the homeless poor into your house; when you see the naked, to cover them, and not to hide yourself from your own kin?

Then your light shall break forth like the dawn, and your healing shall spring up quickly; your vindicator shall go before you, the glory of God shall be your rearguard. God will guide you continually and satisfy your needs in parched places, and make your bones strong; and you shall be like a watered garden, like a spring of water, whose waters never fail.

Your ancient ruins shall be rebuilt; you shall raise up the foundations of many generations; you shall be called the repairer of the breach, the restorer of streets to live in.

From *The Message*, an adaptation by Eugene Peterson

This is the kind of fast day I'm after: to break the chains of injustice, get rid of exploitation in the workplace, free the oppressed, cancel debts. What I'm interested in seeing you do is sharing your food with the hungry, inviting the homeless poor into your homes, putting clothes on the shivering ill-clad, being available to your own families. Do this and the lights will turn on, and your lives will turn around at once.

You'll be like a well-watered garden, a gurgling spring that never runs dry. You'll use the old rubble of past lives to build anew, rebuild the foundations from out of your past. You'll be known as those who can fix anything, restore old ruins, rebuild and renovate, make the community livable again.

"I Have a Dream," Martin Luther King, Jr.

I have a dream today… that every valley shall be exalted, and every hill and mountain shall be made low, the rough places will be made plain, and the crooked places will be made straight; and the glory of the Lord shall be revealed and all flesh shall see it together.

ℰℐ

THESE ARE STRONG visions! The dreams of Martin Luther King and the proclamations of Isaiah paint pictures of an ideal world. Such visions and longings are found throughout scripture, from the portrait of the Garden of Eden to the prophecy of Revelation, so beautifully echoed by the hymn-writer:

> O holy city, seen of John, where Christ, the Lamb, doth reign,
> Within whose foursquare walls shall come no night, nor need,
>   nor pain,
> And where the tears are wiped from eyes that shall not weep
>   again! (Bowie)

But the world to which we awaken these mornings is *not* the realized dream of Martin Luther King's world of peace through non-violence. We don't enjoy the fullness of creation that the Bible tells us was God's design – the perfection of Eden, or the order and comfort of the Revelation vision.

Rather, war, oppression, the growing global divisions between rich and poor, and greedy consumption of resources characterize our world. Even in the church, we are all too familiar with infighting, inward focus, and a numb resignation to our world's plight. We seek sanctuary rather than working to realize the vision.

But the words of the prophets and the ministry of Jesus call us to right wrongs, to stem injustice, to rebuild what is destroyed. We're called to work toward this vision that seems like utopia.

Utopia, we learn from Plato's *Republic* and Sir Thomas More, is a "place" – for some writers, a physical space; for others, a spiritual state of being – a place free from hunger, war and suffering, filled with beauty.

The word *utopia* seems to be a play on Greek words, meaning either "no place" or "good place", or perhaps both. In Greek, *ou-topos* means *no place; eu-topos* means *good place.*

We hear echoes of Eden – life in harmony with all creation. Many philosophies and most religions have stories/myths of a beginning or time past when humankind lived in a state of perfect happiness and fulfillment and in harmony with God or the gods. They also express hope that human beings have the capacity and the desire to restore or work toward this state of social contentment.

Prophets, philosophers, mystics, and the writer of Revelation describe a realized whole, a new creation that replaces the old.

Clearly, this vision is still not fully realized. Each generation makes some movement, progress toward a more peaceful world, a lessening of suffering. Each era's insights have led to new social strategies, but we clearly have work to do!

Do we say that we have failed?

Utopian writer/philosopher Kim Stanley Robinson offers a helpful understanding, another way to hold hope without being unrealistic or succumbing to the fate of failure – utopia as a *process* rather than a received whole. He writes:

> [We] must redefine utopia. It isn't the perfect end-product of our wishes; define it so and it deserves the scorn of those who sneer when they hear the word. No. Utopia is the process of making a better world. (Robinson, 95)

Utopia can only be a process, because brokenness, wounded-ness, and – yes – evil, are human realities.

In his iconic novel *The Time Machine*, H.G. Wells describes an idyllic world, but below this world live the Morlocks, terrible, un-dermining, consciously evil people. The harsh reality is that for any projectable future, we will have our Morlocks. And utopia – as a fully realized way of life – won't exist so long as we have Morlocks.

In the *achieved* sense, the dream of Martin Luther King as a goal, the vision of the kingdom of God as a goal, utopia as a goal – all these make no sense.

Those who have achieved real change in the world have believed – but not naively. They have been aware and vigilant, knowing that resistance to love and justice is ever-present. They have heard – and even preached – the sermon. They've seen the vision, been to the mountain top and seen the Promised Land. But it hasn't been a city on a hill in the sweet by and by. It hasn't been a miraculous creation of a utopian god.

Rather, those who have made real change in the world have known the Morlocks. And they have faced the discouraging possi-bility that the poor will always be with us. Those who can imagine a world of hope and peace are motivated by both realities, as the wind of the Spirit has invigorated their kind, bold action for change.

The prophet Amos, Jesus, Gandhi, King. You know their names. These are not naïve preachers of a kingdom in the sky, not immature activists who deny the existence of those who live in contention and revel in power over others. Yet they know somehow that utopia lives in the journey, in each day's kindnesses, in each strengthened relationship. Each hungry soul fed with supportive touch. Each message of justice spoken – and then actually lived.

Utopia, the dream, the Realm of God, lives in what you do and say each day. What you do matters – to this community, to

God and to the very real state of the world. What this congregation does – little things, big things – matters and is the utopian realm of God. It's what Jesus preached and lived. He didn't just say, for example, that the world would be set right with gender equality; he touched and spoke to women and empowered them to act with moral authority. In that moment, the realm of God broke through.

He didn't just say that non-Jews had access to Yahweh; he told the story of a Samaritan who brought God's healing to the supposedly chosen one. The one excluded and on the margins was recognized as holy. In that moment, the world was right; the realm of God was known.

He didn't just say that all deserved to eat; he fed and blessed all who were hungry. They experienced it – knew it was real – in the doing of it.

In 1996, the city of Atlanta, Georgia, was preparing for the summer Olympic Games. One of the venues was in a neighboring county that was openly and proudly homophobic. So a group of local activists and pastors arranged a protest to challenge the Olympic committee to move the events out of Cobb County. I was shocked when another minister in the city refused to participate. He explained his refusal with what was, for him, a rhetorical question: *"What does this have to do with Jesus?"* My friends, it has everything to do with Jesus! Our mandate as followers of Christ is to relieve suffering, to release the chains that bind. That's what the church does. That's what Jesus commissioned us to do to bring in the realm of God, the vision of prophets old and new.

If we root ourselves in the gospel – that is, in following Jesus' ways of seeking God, of caring for the poor, of attending to those closest to him, of challenging hypocrisy, of touching the untouchable – the realm of God lives in us. Then our salvific visions of lions lying down with lambs, of rebuilding cities and feeding the hungry, can build the sort of utopia that Jesus created around himself and that he called us to build.

This is not a vision that can be done once and for all. It isn't something that God proclaims and so it's accomplished – a magic heaven. It isn't something that's so perfect that we know we'll never see it in our lifetime – rather it's a world of righteousness and justice that can exist when we live rightly and justly. Do you get it? We are called to be it – right in the middle of the world in which we live.

And now is the time, the only time. In his *Letter from Birmingham Jail*, Dr King wrote to those who urged him to wait to insist on justice:

"I have almost reached the regrettable conclusion that the Negro's great stumbling block in [the] stride toward freedom is… the white moderate… who paternalistically believes he can set the timetable for another's freedom." (King, *Letter*, 84)

Dr King preached:

"I have a dream today… that every valley shall be exalted, and every hill and mountain shall be made low, the rough places will be made plain, and the crooked places will be made straight; and the glory of the Lord shall be revealed and all flesh shall see it together." (King, "I Have a Dream," 122)

The vision. The utopia. The salvation. The word that longs, in the imagination of God, to become flesh in us.

May it be so.

8

LIKE TREES

Luke 6:20-26

Then he looked up at his disciples and said: "Blessed are you who are poor, for yours is the kingdom of God.

"Blessed are you who are hungry now, for you will be filled. Blessed are you who weep now, for you will laugh.

"Blessed are you when people hate you, and when they exclude you, revile you, and defame you on account of the [Human One]. Rejoice on that day and leap for joy, for surely your reward is great in heaven; for that is what their ancestors did to the prophets.

"But woe to you who are rich, for you have received your consolation. Woe to you who are full now, for you will be hungry. Woe to you who are laughing now, for you will mourn and weep. Woe to you when all speak well of you, for that is what their ancestors did to the false prophets."

❧

IN THE VERY FIRST psalm, we hear words that are similar to these wisdom words from Jeremiah and from Jesus:

> Happy are those who do not take the path that sinners tread, those whose delight is in God's law. They are like trees planted by streams of water, which yield their fruit in its season, and their leaves do not wither. (Psalm 1:1-3)

Jeremiah says that these trees "send out their roots by the stream and even in drought, they do not cease to bear fruit." (Jeremiah 17:8)

This is the guiding image for today: a tree that is planted by a stream rather than in a desert, where the roots would not grow deep; a tree whose roots sink deep into the earth for nourishment; a tree planted by ever-flowing streams; a tree that continues to flourish even when rain is scarce, when heat threatens to wither its leaves.

This is the goal, I believe, of our text for today: to call us to be people who put our roots deep into the being of God. Reflection on the text invites us to ask: Where are we grounded? How are we nourished? What fruit do we produce? Are we rooted in the desert or by streams of water? What in our living indicates where we've rooted ourselves?

Jesus speaks of being blessed or cursed. This is Luke's version of the more familiar beatitudes that are part of the Sermon on the Mount in the fifth chapter of Matthew's gospel. Beatitudes simply means blessings – and that's what Matthew includes – blessings with no curses or woes.

But that's just one of the important differences in these two accounts of similar teachings of Jesus. Matthew tells us of the Sermon on the Mount; Luke, on the other hand, describes a Sermon on the Plain. In Luke's telling of these teachings, Jesus is not removed from, higher than, the people. Rather, they move with him and clamor to get closer, to touch him. Matthew has Jesus offer nine blessings and no curses; Luke, four blessings and four woes.

Matthew spiritualizes the blessings, such as "Blessed are the poor in spirit," whereas Luke is much more out there: "Blessed are the poor," he says. Matthew speaks of those who are blessed, while Luke makes Jesus' words a direct address of both blessings and curses: Blessed are *you*; Woe unto *you*. In the Sermon on the Plain, Jesus reminds us that it's *us*, that we are both blessed and cursed, and that the coin of human life in relation to God and each other has two sides.

These sayings of Jesus are both puzzling and troubling. I would like to touch on two blessings and two curses and ask that we look a little deeper and that we don't take our seats just yet on either the blessings side or the woes side. Suspend your own reward or punishment – your state of feeling blessed or cursed – until we take a closer look.

Blessed are you who are poor, for yours is the Realm of God.

I wish Jesus had said more. I wish that he had explained whether this was an observation about people who are poor, or a promise to those who are poor. Blessed are you who are *poor*? Being poor, really poor, and destitute would be unimaginably horrible, real suffering beyond anything most of us can imagine. Those who are poor are often victims of the assumptions of the wealthy.

And yet, most of us know the trappings of money and material things all too well. I don't know about you, but I can feel truly satisfied with what I have until I see a really hot car or a house that I love that's way beyond my means. Something snaps in me that I don't like. Many of us can get sucked in easier than we might like to think.

I've known some really poor people – at least they were poor by modern Western standards. And I can tell you one thing that practically all of them had in common: faith, and the belief that God was their advocate and comforter, their source of life and hope. And their relationship with God wasn't romanticized – just real, coping with what is, with an abiding gratitude for what sustained them.

I struggle with how to talk about those who are poor without observing in a way that objectifies or romanticizes. Knowing a woman named Kim helped me. Kim's husband died suddenly, leaving her with three small children. She was engaged in a constant battle with the landlord of the only flat she could afford, trying to get him to stop water from coming in through the ceiling light fixture. The crack dealers next door were a threat to her adolescent children, and the fear of violence in the neighborhood was always present.

And yet, Kim was so filled with the love and hope of God that I couldn't feel pity for her. I felt fully justified in my burning anger on her behalf, but not pity. And more than that, Kim gave me an incredible gift – a gift of seeing God through her eyes and life. Her priorities and worries were different from mine, and I wanted mine to somehow be more like hers. She had absolutely no greed in her spirit. Her children were embraced by the security of her love and presence, rather than just assuming that life was sustained by the latest gadgets. Her faith was strong and real and practical.

Kim makes me wonder – was Jesus really talking economics? I don't know. I don't think he was saying it's wrong to have money. But maybe there's something intertwined with money or possessions and how we live our lives in relation to God and other people.

Blessed are you who weep now, for you will laugh.

I've seen mourning and weeping; all of us who have lived very long have. And we've felt it, too: that pain that turns us inside out. We can't see the end.

I particularly remember Jake, who was a friend of mine in seminary. Jake's nine-day-old son struggled for his life and lost. The moaning in that hospital room and at that funeral was deep and loud, threatening to take those whose intense pain wracked their bodies and souls into the depths of despair. The anguish was visible on faces and in bodies.

I too have pangs that cut deep into my body when the reality of my dad's death stings again. Loss and pain take residence in our hearts sometimes. But I feel the corners of my mouth lift when I remember the sweet vibrato of my dad's beautiful whistling or find myself doing something exactly like he did. And I'm filled with gratitude and with a joy that is born of experiencing the whole of life. I not only know that it really *is* better to have loved and lost than never to have loved at all. I know, too, that the joy would not be as deep without the mourning. The laughter would have less soul.

And I believe that the life to come will just magnify that reality somehow. Our mourning will turn to dancing, but we wouldn't be inspired to dance unless we had mourned.

Woe to you who are full now, for you will be hungry.

Fullness. Satisfaction. Completeness. Contentment; not looking for more.

When I taught school, I was pretty well convinced that I could deal with anything in my students except apathy. I simply didn't know how to teach students who weren't interested in learning or experiencing something new, who weren't curious. Perhaps this is what Jesus is saying. If we're so full of whatever we stuff ourselves with in response to all the various types of hunger pangs of our lives, there's no room for the work of God, there's no soul space to share what we have with those who need and want it too.

When friends from England visit the United States, they remind me of just how huge the portions of food are that are served in American homes and restaurants, of the often excessive American way of life. Both physically and metaphorically, we can usually eat all we want until we are overly full – without a thought about our health or the hunger of others. How empty! How ironic! What a curse, really.

We can get caught in a pattern of consuming until we can consume no longer, oblivious to those who are without, shuttered to our self-focused consumerism, numb to our growing dissatisfaction.

Many Americans and other Western people regularly overeat. And many of us are seriously overindulged with other things that substitute for vital nourishment. Are we satisfied? Are we filled with that which makes us whole? Are our roots sunk deep into the earth of God, where the richest nutrients await our taproots? Or do we open the refrigerator instead of our hearts?

Woe to you when all speak well of you...

I don't know about you, but being accepted and respected is pretty important to me. The stories of trauma that dominate many of our childhoods are about not being accepted or affirmed for who we are or what we do. But I also know the personal anxiety that results when being liked and praised is the primary goal. The needs of the self that tries to please overtake the real self, and we're lost. The one that God created and loves is lost in our search for the approval that we think we need.

Jesus taught that being a disciple is about having values that far surpass the value of being liked and praised. If that is all we seek, that is all we find. Empty praise. And we become dependent on it. Following Jesus means living for and in the values of love, justice, righteousness, and peace with less regard for the judgment of others – or their praise.

So, my friends, what is Jesus saying to us? Again, hear me: Jesus is *not* saying that it's bad to be rich or full or healthy or have a good reputation. But to think that these are our primary aims in life may cause us to stumble and fall. To mistakenly pursue these aims as our first priority, or to root ourselves in them expecting sustenance, or to focus exclusively on our own satisfaction, is a curse indeed.

Do we live in such a way that our roots are in goods or our career or our comfort? Do we have a sense of fullness that numbs us to a longing for God? Do we just assume that we can rely on the advantages that we have for life's meaning and fulfillment? Do we feel self-sufficient or appear self-absorbed, oblivious to the needs of others? What do we do to make life better for others? Do we continue to reach out when things aren't going well for us? Do our lives bear "fruit", the fruit that Jesus talks about: love, joy, peace, patience, kindness, goodness, faithfulness, gentleness, and self-control?

Let's take a look in our souls today, take a hard, realistic look. My guess is that all of us will find that we're not squarely on one side or the other: we're rich and poor, overindulged and hungry, weeping and laughing, dependent on the praise of others and held in God's love for us. We're acclaimed and shamed and somewhere in between.

Can we own both sides? Can we know that we're both self and shadow? Can we open ourselves to those blessings that will ground us in love, put our roots into the ground of life? Are we willing to be fully conscious of our human capacity to choose to live either in the way of blessing or feeding at the trough of life's trappings?

We can freely choose to plant ourselves by the river of life. Indeed, Jesus seems to say that when we realize and live out of the realization of our vulnerability and need, we'll put our roots down deep.

We can connect with the source of meaning and life. We can produce the fruit that we really long for.

Imagine that tree; it's you – deeply rooted in the presence and nature of God. And no matter how hard the wind blows or how violent our world becomes, our roots are deep and connected to the Source of Life.

> They shall be like a tree planted by the water, sending out its
>   roots by the stream.
> It shall not fear when heat comes, and its leaves shall stay green;
>   in the year of drought it is not anxious, and it does not cease
>   to bear fruit. (Jeremiah 17:8)

Allow God to search your heart today. And dare to put your roots down deep.

9

DREAM ON!

Black History Month

The Dreams of Parent and Child from Genesis 28:10-17 and 36:3-11, from *The Message*, an adaptation by Eugene Peterson

The Parent's Dream

Jacob left Beersheba and went to Haran. He came to a certain place and camped for the night since the sun had set. He took one of the stones there, set it under his head and lay down to sleep. And he dreamed: A stairway was set on the ground and it reached all the way to the sky; angels of God were going up and going down on it.

Then God was right before Jacob, saying, "I am Yahweh, the God of your ancestors: Abraham and Sarah, Isaac and Rebekah. I'm giving the ground on which you are sleeping to you and to your descendants. Your descendants will be as the dust of the Earth; they'll stretch from west to east and from north to south. All the families of the Earth will bless themselves in you and your descendants. Yes. I'll stay with you, I'll protect you, and I'll bring you back to this very ground. I'll stay with you until I've done everything I promised."

Jacob woke up from his sleep. He said, "God is in this place. And I didn't even know it!" Jacob was terrified and whispered in awe, "Incredible. Wonderful. Holy."

The Child's Dream

Joseph, Jacob's son, had a dream. When he told it to his brothers, they hated him.

Joseph said, "Listen to this dream I had. We were all out in the field gathering bundles of wheat. All of a sudden my bundle stood straight up and your bundles circled around it and bowed down to mine." His brothers said, "So! You're going to rule us? You're going to boss us around?" And they hated him more than ever because of his dreams and the way he talked.

He had another dream and told this one also to his brothers: "I dreamed another dream – the sun and moon and eleven stars bowed down to me!"

When Joseph told his father about the dream, Jacob reprimanded him: "What's with all this dreaming? Am I and your mother and your brothers all supposed to bow down to you?" Now his brothers were really jealous; but his father brooded over the whole business.

℃↻

WE CELEBRATE Black History Month at Decatur United Church of Christ because it's important to all of us: in honoring the history of African-American people, we give voice to those whose lives have been silenced and yet have shaped our nation in many ways, and we do a little to put history right.

In educating ourselves, we find inspiration from the power of the human spirit, pride in the heritage of liberation that we all have received from the struggle for human dignity. We learn more deeply about prayer and desperation, about resistance to oppression, and the quest for freedom. In the story of suffering and triumph, faith and faltering, courage and fear, we all can find our own stories and inspiration to rise up over that which enslaves.

And, in the stories and speeches and sermons of this history, we learn about God. About the God who created all human beings for freedom and dignity, for grace and for giving.

We may assume that sermons and songs during Black History Month will be about freedom and liberation, that they'll be "social justice sermons", but if we simply put them in this category, we may fail to hear the messages of personal piety – messages about relationship with God. We may fail to hear the call to personal ethics, to examine how we behave in the world. Only when we hear these aspects of the message can we hear adequately the call to social righteousness, the call to act for God's justice and peace.

Dreams are visions that embody hopes. Dreams make it possible to perceive what is yet to be.

Dreams are signs of life, of health and possibility.

Dreamers embrace a future – perhaps even an unimaginable, unlikely future – as if it could be so, as if a brighter day has already begun. Dreaming creates the possibility, launches the notion that change can happen, that what is *not* just might be.

The Bible, particularly the Hebrew Bible, is chock-full of dreamers. They call them prophets so we won't think they're totally bonkers. You remember them: Ezekiel, Daniel, Joshua, Joseph.

In the scriptures (and perhaps still), dreams are visions from the Spirit. They're revelations that make it possible to see in that sub-conscious eye what seems beyond reach in the wide-awake world.

The patriarch Jacob is a dreamer. Or he became a dreamer. From the moment of his birth, Jacob was less-than, the second-born twin. Esau, his twin brother – first to be born – had it all. Esau, the eldest, manly one, was favored by his father. All signs pointed to Esau being the one chosen by God to lead the people, to carry on in his father's footsteps, and his father's before him.

Jacob, the quiet, younger twin, struggled to find his place, to be somebody by any means. He bargained and tricked to compete – all morals aside – to get what he longed for. His name even means "one who strives".

But then, he began to dream. Not surprisingly, his dreams were about access and worthiness and struggle for blessing: dreams of a stairway to heaven, of wrestling with God – and not letting go until he receives God's blessing.

God spoke to Jacob in dreams. In the Jacob's Ladder dream, God chose him! God reversed the obvious choice and promised to bless the world through this unlikely brother. The voice of Yahweh said to him: "I am the God of your ancestors; I will give the land on which you lie to you and your descendants."

Before this night, before the dream, Jacob thought he had to work or pretend to be like Esau – something other than what he was – to be blessed.

Jacob was the one from the underside of life, where resentments and shame reside. And yet, God came to him in a dream and made a promise, a promise that he would be set free from his limitations, from his second-class status, a promise that made him both blessed and blessing.

Joseph was Jacob's youngest son. And a dreamer. You heard his dreams: visions of the younger rising up above the elder – son above father. Again, the less likely over the obvious choice.

And – did you notice? Jacob, Joseph's father who was once a dreamer of similar dreams, had a bit of fear that the dream could once again mean that God would turn the tables. Once Jacob had power and hope and identity, he seemed to want everything to stay in that order. Listen:

> "What's with all this dreaming? Am I and your mother and your brothers all supposed to bow down to you?" Now his brothers were really jealous; but his father brooded over the whole business. (Genesis 36:11)

God has more to reveal from the ones who are deemed of lower status.

Against all odds, oppressed people, last-and-least people, dream!

The dream of God – that those of low status will be lifted – comes to life again and again. While being called a "brutish sort of people", some African-American people in early America had the spirit and fire to dream of freedom and the audacity to speak those dreams to life. To overestimate the future.

Dreams are motivating – for both the dreamer and those who are inspired by the dreams. Dreams move to action and call us forward.

African-American history is steeped in dreams – dreams expressed in poetry and song, in anger and protest and resistance, in sermon and story.

The people of the dream have passed it on, and given their lives for it. It has shaped the identity of a people who once were not a people. The dream – sometimes deferred, sometimes left for dead. As James Weldon Johnson expressed in what some call the Black National Anthem:

Stony the road we trod, bitter the chastening rod,
felt in the days when hope unborn had died.

And yet, by the power and priorities of God, the dream survived. And it has changed the world.

Today, we remember a few of the dreamers.

Sojourner Truth had a dream.
Sojourner Truth was born a slave in New York around 1797. She was slave to five masters until, when she was twenty-eight, New York abolished slavery.

Isabella (that was her birth name) had a dream. The dream, the vision, affected her profoundly, leading her – as she later described it – to develop a "perfect trust in God and prayer." (McKissack)

With the dream and a new name – Sojourner Truth – she walked throughout the countryside, speaking and singing about her life and her relationship with God. Imagine it! A newly freed slave. A woman. Traveling alone with only this God-implanted dream!

She eventually joined the Northampton Association, where the realization of her dream grew. There she worked alongside others for abolition, equality, and peace. This former slave – a woman who never learned to read or write – influenced many by following her dream, including President Abraham Lincoln and abolitionist Frederick Douglass.

Frederick Douglass had a dream.

A dream of freedom.

Born into slavery in February of 1818 on Maryland's eastern shore, Douglass's dream was so strong that it led him to repeated attempts to escape, even after being jailed and beaten for trying.

During his early childhood, he was exposed to the horrors of slavery, witnessing brutal whippings, suffering himself from cold and hunger, being sold away and separated from his mother. When he was eight years old, he was sent to Baltimore to serve in the home of a ship builder. There he learned to read and – through his reading – discovered the word *abolition*. "Going to live at Baltimore," Douglass said later, "laid the foundation, and opened the gateway." The seed of the dream was planted; he glimpsed the possibility of freedom.

Frederick finally escaped to New York when he was twenty – his dream realized. But he held the dream for many others who were still suffering. He dared to dream of a day when the American Constitution would be a document of freedom for African-Americans and for women.

He gave his life to promoting that dream. His inspiring rhetoric changed minds and hearts and especially challenged the church to dream that dream that is its heritage, its bedrock.

To turn from self-serving behaviour and call for equality and freedom.

Howard Thurman had a dream.

He said that "a dream is the bearer of a new possibility, the enlarged horizon, the great hope." (Thurman, Morehouse)

Howard Thurman was born in 1899 in Daytona Beach, Florida, and grew up in the segregated South. After graduating as valedictorian from Morehouse College, he was ordained in the Baptist church. He went on to earn a doctorate in theology, studying philosophy and Christian mysticism.

In his book, *Footprints of a Dream*, he tells the story of his radical dream, a dream to build a congregation that was comprised of people from many races, cultures, and faiths – the first congregation in the United States with this diversity. He could envision a church that was unified, spiritually transforming and transformative.

Now, imagine this: his dream was realized in San Francisco in 1944, with the establishment of The Church for the Fellowship of All Peoples. Dr. Thurman served as co-pastor with a white minister.

And Howard Thurman shared his dream, inspiring others to dream, including Reverend Martin Luther King, Jr., whose pastor father was a close friend.

Myles Horton had a dream.

It was, in some ways, like Jacob's dream. He, too, saw a stairway to heaven – a possibility of elevating those who were without pride or hope. A God-dream. Even though Myles Horton was a white man, his dream is *the* dream that is a gravitational center of Black history.

Horton, the grandson of illiterate Tennessee mountain folk, was born in 1905. His working-class parents taught him about love, service, work, and the value of education. His mother's faith planted the dream in his soul: "God is love, and therefore you love your neighbors."

Horton said that:

> If you believe that people are of worth, you can't treat anybody inhumanely, and that means you not only have to love and respect people, but you have to build a society that works on the principle of equality. (Horton, 7)

While studying theology at Union Seminary in New York, a dream was brewing inside him, calling him to develop a school. This school would empower people to deal with problems of inequality – to know their God-given dignity and ability through culture, art, music, and reconciliation skills.

In 1932, he founded The Highlander School in Tennessee, initially to address labor struggles. But it was through the civil rights movement of the 1950s that Highlander gained public attention. It was there that the song "We Shall Overcome" became an integral part of the movement. And it was there that Rosa Parks, Martin Luther King Jr., and Andrew Young learned the ways of non-violent protest.

The dream lived on through Myles Horton. From the heart of the scriptures, in an unlikely place, the dream continued.

And Martin Luther King, Jr. had a dream.

We know the words. And we know their worth.

The flame of the dream, the flame of hope, has been passed. The torch is carried with courage and power. And bit by bit, the dream of God – that those who are considered low are lifted up, chosen, treasured, gifted – is coming to life.

As we celebrate Black History Month, we celebrate the Dream

and the dreamers. We celebrate those whose dreams inspired other dreamers, and those who gave life and courage to the dream.

We remember those who lived Audre Lorde's words:

> When I dare to be powerful – to use my strength in the service of my vision, then it becomes less and less important whether I am afraid. (Lorde, 13)

And we celebrate the dream-giver, the God who comes to those that the world least expects – those on the bottom rungs of the ladder – to inspire hope and create vision, so that the world might be saved.

How are we to respond? By daring to dream. And by passing it on.

Do you have a dream today?

Dream on! Dream on!

LENT

10

THIRST

John 4:5-15

So Jesus came to a Samaritan city called Sychar, near the plot of ground that Jacob had given to his son Joseph. Jacob's well was there, and Jesus, tired out by his journey, was sitting by the well. It was about noon. A Samaritan woman came to draw water, and Jesus said to her, "Give me a drink." (His disciples had gone to the city to buy food.) The Samaritan woman said to him, "How is it that you, a Jew, ask a drink of me, a woman of Samaria?" (Jews do not share things in common with Samaritans.) Jesus answered her, "If you knew the gift of God, and who it is that is saying to you, 'Give me a drink,' you would have asked him, and he would have given you living water." The woman said to him, "Sir, you have no bucket, and the well is deep. Where do you get that living water? Are you greater than our ancestor Jacob, who gave us the well, and with his sons and his flocks drank from it?" Jesus said to her, "Everyone who drinks of this water will be thirsty again, but those who drink of the water that I will give them will never be thirsty. The water that I will give will become in them a spring of water gushing up to eternal life." The woman said to him, "Sir, give me this water, so that I may never be thirsty or have to keep coming here to draw water."

ↀ

A TIME OF intentional contemplation, Lent is about getting down to what matters in our connection with God. Lent calls us into the wilderness, the interior place of aloneness, danger, introspection. This is the territory of wandering and reckoning. A journey into Lent's wilderness may reveal some harsh realities of life to us, making us ready – through need and desperate longing – for resurrection.

One of the wonders of choosing to spend time in Lent's wilderness is that we begin to realize our thirst, our need. Face to face with our fears, our brokenness, our screwed-up priorities, we thirst. We need to drink relief, forgiveness, acceptance. Our souls need to be invited to sip a healing elixir, to be poured a cup of salvation.

During my childhood, I remember only a few of my parents' books. Two things stand out in my mental bookshelf perusal: my father's *National Geographic* magazines with photographs that beckoned me to faraway places, and a little devotional book by Mrs. Charles Cowman that my mother kept on the end table with her Bible. The title of this book that was clearly integral to her spiritual reading intrigued me. It seemed like a contradiction, an impossibility: *Streams in the Desert*. Water in the wilderness, streams in the desert, speaks of the deepest need for survival. Simultaneously, the notion seems impossible.

Now, the text tells us that Jesus had to go through Samaria. Even if the course to his destination didn't require him to travel through Samaria, his mission demanded it. Love required him to travel to the edge.

Samaritans, as we know, were despised, considered a mongrel race of half-Jews. The hatred and rivalry between Jews and Samaritans was about religion, race, and class. Each would have said the other was illegitimate, and its members perhaps even sub-human. Because of racial tension, Samaritans did not even go to Jerusalem to worship in the temple.

Jesus went to Jacob's well – in Samaria. While he was there, a Samaritan woman came to the well about noon. This may seem unexceptional, but the normal time for women to fetch water from wells was early morning when the temperatures were cool, and so that they would have water to begin the day. So, her arrival there in the heat of the day signals some extraordinary circumstance.

Perhaps she came to the well at noon out of shame or guilt, to avoid the reproach of others. The fact that she is unnamed could be a sign of her lack of importance, or it could suggest that she represents a particular type of woman. But imagine her surprise when she comes in this off-hour with her water bucket balanced on her head, and encounters a stranger, a Jewish man, sitting beside the well.

The conversation that ensued is the longest conversation with Jesus of any told in the gospels.

Jesus' initiation of this conversation is simply not proper behavior, given the boundaries of gender and race. A Jewish man would not strike up a dialogue with a Samaritan woman, much less one of suspect character. But he did – and he asked her for a drink. He even drank after her.

This conjures up images of segregated water fountains in the Southern United States until the early 1970s. For a white person to drink from a fountain marked for "colored" people would have been unimaginable. This seems like a similar boundary-crossing action.

Jesus broke all the taboos and said to her: "If you knew the gift of God and who it is that asks you for a drink, you would have asked and he would have given you living water."

Then she talked back, with both impudence and interest: "Sir, you have nothing to draw with and the well is deep. Where can you get this living water?"

Jesus answered, "Everyone who drinks this water will be thirsty again, but whoever drinks the water I give will never thirst."

The woman said to him, "Sir, give me this water so I won't get thirsty and have to keep coming here to draw water." Her emotional and spiritual thirst calls out louder now, her thirst for safety and relief from shame, for peace and acceptance. She wasn't simply asking for labor-saving water collection. Rather, she longed for a life of love and acceptance, without being humiliated and excluded.

Later in this fifth chapter of John, it turns out that the woman's life is a mess, especially in regard to her series of husbands. But we don't know her situation, only her reputation. Was she without options, singled repeatedly by death or the divorces that husbands could easily pronounce? Did she then struggle through the ensuing disgrace and isolation, with no secure place, without a husband, managing to survive in any way she could?

Maybe she had no fresh cuts or bruises, but Jesus saw plenty of wounds in her. He saw that she yearned for a sense of self, for belonging, for identity, for the living water of kindness and compassion, dignity and hope. She longed to be whole again, but she had accepted the only substitutes she knew. She had tried avoiding those who would taunt her, keeping her head down and her profile low, even suffering in the heat to achieve relative spiritual and emotional safety.

Jesus saw and had compassion. He reached past the divide of Jew and Samaritan, of female and male, past judgments and hatred, and offered her the acceptance and relief of God, which isn't dependent on who you are, what you've done, any place or ancestry or set of rules. He appealed to her ability to make moral decisions for herself. He reached right for her thirst.

I wonder if the living water and having five husbands could

both represent the search for the "real thing", for that which will satisfy.

We are steeped in a culture of deceptive advertising, aren't we? Remember the soda advertisement that said, "Obey your thirst?" Do you hear the irony? Tapping into a deep primal human need for water, the ad says, "obey your thirst," suggesting that if you chug down some of their soda instead of water, your thirst will be quenched, your need will be met. And as we drink much of it in, we just become more and more thirsty.

Are you accepting substitutes for living water, that is, the real thing which will content your heart, offer you a way of life in peace and honesty, dignity, depth of joy?

We try all sorts of remedies to relieve our thirst for acceptance, for love, for meaning to our lives, but nothing short of an encounter with Love itself will do – nothing short of a drink of that cup will satisfy.

The character and nature of that Love – of God – is like the character of water. We know that metaphor well enough that it speaks to our souls: "As the deer pants for the water, so my soul longs after you," chants the psalmist.

Images of water speak of God. The very opening words of Genesis offer their poetic words of creation: "The spirit of God moved upon the face of the waters and brought life." (Genesis 1:2)

The voice of Allah speaks from the pages of the Qur'an: "We have created every living thing from water." (Sura 21, The Prophets, ayat 30)

And the Exodus, that narrative of God's liberation, tells us that the people crossed the sea from slavery into freedom. (Exodus 14)

The gospel of John practically makes a study of water and God: Jesus teaches Nicodemus about being born of water and Spirit; the man who had waited near the pool for healing for thirty-eight years is immersed and healed; and this woman at the well is offered living water.

Water cleanses, heals, sustains life. Its tides and currents hold the pulse of life. Water, like Spirit, is ubiquitous – both inside and outside of us. Water is an agent of change: it dilutes, erodes, saturates.

"Give me this living water," she said.

That water of life, the living water that satisfies, comes in many forms. Theologian Dorothee Soelle recalls her acquaintance with Dorothy Day, the passionate and rebellious founder of the Catholic Worker Movement. Dorothy Day worked tirelessly in her thirst for justice and peace, with and on behalf of the poorest of the poor. And sometimes, when the wilderness was dark and deep, she would withdraw from her work and from her friends and cry – for days. She would sit alone, eat nothing and just cry – long and bitterly.

And then, as if fed by her tears, she would find strength to continue. She found the water of life in tears – a depth of prayer and consolation. (Soelle, *Silent Cry*, 252)

What drink did Jesus offer the Samaritan woman? He told the truth of her life – it's all out in the open here. And right in the middle of the sordid truth, without a damning word, he offered her the cup of grace and dignity. Some would simply call it "salvation". Others might say she drank from the cup of unconditional love and acceptance and that God's love transformed her. I wonder if Jesus gave her the cup of her life back – her dignity and personhood. Perhaps we could say that she was born again – of water and Spirit.

Drinking the cup of life, Henri Nouwen proposes, is fully appropriating and internalizing our own unique existence, with all its sorrows and joys. It is not easy to do this. We might not feel capable of accepting our own life; we might keep fighting for a different life. Often a deep protest against our "fate" rises in us:

> We wish we were in another body, living in another time, or had another mind… But as we finally come to befriend our own reality, we can move beyond our protest, put the cup of our life to our lips and drink it. (Nouwen, *Can You Drink the Cup?*, 87)

Perhaps this is what the woman did that day: drank the cup of her own life. Touched by the acceptance of God that Jesus offered, she saw the possibility of befriending her own life, of claiming it as her own, with its struggles, mistakes, and opportunities; and drinking more deeply of it than she thought possible.

Like this woman, many of us realize the substitutions we've made: money, friends, education, sex, self-sufficiency, substances, success, excitement, career, even religion or God-talk. Why is it that some of us need to try everything imaginable before we open our hearts to the Spirit, realizing that it's that sustaining Spirit that we've craved all along?

We, too, are offered this living water. We can be drenched with the Spirit of God, filled with the water of life. And we are called to follow the welcoming way of Jesus at the well, to offer living water to those who thirst: to greet, to touch, to comfort, to include, to confront, to lift up, to bring promise and possibility, to empower others to drink the cup of hope.

Are you thirsty for peace and hope and purpose? Think it's impossible – either because you've tried to no avail or because you think somehow that you don't deserve it? Are you tired of accepting substitutes, trying to satisfy your deep inner thirst to no avail?

If we just keep tasting what's on offer, we think we'll eventually find what satisfies. Or, we may have stopped hoping years ago, stifled the need to the point that we've forgotten what we long for.

We may have put layers of protection around our hearts to guard against any more disappointment.

But God's love is a deep well that never runs dry. All it needs is a thirsty soul. You see, the only criterion for receiving it is that we thirst for it. That's it. Perhaps you feel you've messed up your life one time too many and so God's Living Water is somehow not available to you. Or you think you believe the wrong things – or don't believe at all.

You know… Jesus didn't seem to care about if or what the Samaritan woman believed. He just knew she was thirsty!

Lent gives us permission to be thirsty. It invites us to be thirsty. It assures us that God is thirsty for us. This story invites us to drink deeply from the water of life.

We've heard the testimonies of those who have been satisfied. May we, too, drink deeply of God – that we may live and thrive.

May it be so.

EASTER

11

STOLEN?

John 20:1-18

Early on the first day of the week, while it was still dark, Mary Magdalene came to the tomb and saw that the stone had been removed from the tomb. So she ran and went to Simon Peter and the other disciple, the one whom Jesus loved, and said to them, "They have taken the Lord out of the tomb, and we do not know where they have laid him." Then Peter and the other disciple set out and went toward the tomb. The two were running together, but the other disciple outran Peter and reached the tomb first. He bent down to look in and saw the linen wrappings lying there, but he did not go in. Then Simon Peter came, following him, and went into the tomb. He saw the linen wrappings lying there, and the cloth that had been on Jesus' head, not lying with the linen wrappings but rolled up in a place by itself. Then the other disciple, who reached the tomb first, also went in, and he saw and believed; for as yet they did not understand the scripture, that he must rise from the dead. Then the disciples returned to their homes.

But Mary stood weeping outside the tomb. As she wept, she bent over to look into the tomb; and she saw two angels in white, sitting where the body of Jesus had been lying, one at the head and the other at the feet. They said to her, "Woman, why are you weeping?" She said to them, "They have taken away my Lord, and I do not know where they have laid him." When she had said this, she turned around and saw Jesus standing there, but she did not know that it was Jesus. Jesus said to her, "Woman, why are you weeping? Who are you looking for?"

Supposing him to be the gardener, she said to him, "Sir, if you have carried him away, tell me where you have laid him, and I will take him away." Jesus said to her,

"Mary!" She turned and said to him in Hebrew, "Rabbouni!" (which means Teacher). Jesus said to her, "Do not hold on to me, because I have not yet ascended... But go to my brothers and say to them, 'I am ascending... to my God and your God.'" Mary Magdalene went and announced to the disciples, "I have seen the Lord"; and she told them that he had said these things to her.

❧

ALMOST EVERY YEAR, major magazines publish articles about the last days of Jesus, the crucifixion, or the possibility of resurrection. Headlines from *Time* alone include: "Did It Really Happen? Can We Still Believe in Miracles?", "Was Jesus' Resurrection a Sequel?", "Why Did Jesus Have To Die?", and "Resurrection: A Jew Looks at Jesus."

The theme for this year [2010] seems to be the shroud of Turin and the search for resurrection evidence. The History Channel premiered a series entitled *The Real Face of Jesus*, based on computer graphics and the shroud; and Pope Benedict reopened speculations about the shroud when he declared that it is the authentic burial garment of Jesus.

When we last met, on Good Friday, all hope was lost. At least it looked that way. Jesus had refused to placate the Roman government, refused to stop advocating for those on the margins, refused to put the law before the needs of people. And people were listening and following. Jesus threatened the power of Rome, and they'd had enough. So, on Friday, Jesus was crucified. Dead. Buried. It was over.

No one anticipated or hoped for a resurrection. They knew, as we do, that things like that simply don't happen. They had seen death before; they knew its finality, its ultimate power. Dead people stay dead, and death is where the story ends.

Today's narrative begins early on Sunday morning while it was still dark. And in that liminal, mystical space between light and dark, events unfolded that were beyond imagination.

Mary Magdalene, according to John, was first at the tomb. But she wasn't thinking resurrection; she came to grieve, to be close to the one she loved. But she found the stone rolled away, the tomb empty.

Mary, that unlikely witness to the empty tomb that would change the world, ran from the garden to find Jesus' friends, to report that "they" had taken Jesus' body. Mary didn't say where "they" had taken it, or who "they" were. "They have taken away my Lord, and I do not know where they have laid him."

When Peter and John came to the tomb, they found the abandoned shroud that had wrapped Jesus' body. The immediate assumption was body-snatching, even though the burial clothes had been removed and neatly folded, which might seem to contradict that scenario.

After this disturbing discovery, the disciples went back to their homes, and Mary remained weeping outside the tomb. They seemed resigned to their belief that someone had taken the body of Jesus. At least until that intimate encounter when Mary experienced all the evidence she needed that he had not been stolen. Jesus spoke to her, called her by name, shone with the love that even death could not hold. Surely the worry of a stolen Jesus never plagued her again!

The question that I bring this Easter Sunday is not whether Jesus rose from the grave two thousand years ago. Nor do I ask if it's possible that someone stole his body. Rather, my question for today, for myself and for each of you, is this: What does this have to do with us here and now? Theft or resurrection, how do we hear this story today?

It seems to me that the possibility of Jesus getting stolen continues. When I hear claims that Jesus would oppose every American having access to healthcare, when Jesus is used to justify homophobia or racism or sexism, when the gospel is relegated to some notion of salvation that favors the rich over the poor, or when Christians dismiss or even vilify those whose spiritual experience is not identical to theirs, it seems to me that Jesus has indeed been stolen. He is stolen and buried in doctrine, in cultures of self-serving, fear, and prejudice.

And we cry in despair with Mary, "They have taken away my lord." Those who present Jesus as maintainer of the status quo have taken away this radical, love-at-all-cost risk-taker. They've tamed him and made him respectable, shut him away from those who need him most. In these days when Jesus seems taken and used for the agendas of modern empires, when his own ethic of love and justice is co-opted by those in power, what can lead us to renewed Easter hope? Can the transforming way of Christ still live in spite of all that opposes or perverts it?

I think you'd agree with me that we as individuals, in the church and beyond, need resurrection. We need something to bring life from death. We're all too aware that death, oppression, depression, betrayal, hopelessness, dread and suffering work their destruction in our present day. We need resurrection hope today, not a stolen Jesus.

What could bring us this power of love and life that we need so desperately? Is Jesus too far gone into the realms of the powerful to make a difference? What sort of resurrection would it take to bring back this Jesus of radical love and challenge?

A Mary Experience would make all the difference. That intimate encounter with Jesus is all the evidence Mary needed and it's the evidence we need as well. You see, the stealing of Jesus, whether a first-century theory or a contemporary religious and social reality, becomes irrelevant when Jesus calls our name. When the love and justice of Jesus come alive in this world, we see Jesus and know that he will not be stolen, then or now.

The stealing of Jesus by literalism and violent fundamentalism is rampant and virulent in a number of African countries. In Nigeria, both Christian and Muslim officials pursue and prosecute Christian transgender and gay people who assert that God loves them as they are. In Kenya, even parents, in the name of Jesus, turn over their gay children to be imprisoned and tortured. Jesus is stolen.

But Michael Kimindu, a priest in Nairobi, is witness to resurrection. His life and work are proof that Jesus cannot be stolen, but is alive. Michael, a heterosexual man, challenges the church, speaks with the voice of Jesus, claiming God's love for those excluded. When he speaks, when he saves lives and offers hope, Christ is risen again, and then again and again as those who felt destined to imprisonment and death are given life anew. Contained in neither tomb nor torture, many encounter Jesus the Liberator, and a stolen Jesus is reclaimed.

Singer/songwriter Marsha Stevens tells of the horrors of her childhood. During bouts of her parents' drunken fights, she would hide away, waiting for the violence to end.

But she was never alone. The "man behind the couch" would stay with her, wait with her and, in a way, protect her. Later, she explains that she "recognized" the man behind the couch as the Jesus of whom the church speaks. She had already known his presence and knew that he was with her.

This resurrection experience is what we sing about in her famous song, "For Those Tears I Died":

You said you'd come and share all my sorrow;
You said you'd be there for all my tomorrows.
I know you are thirsty – you won't be denied.

Even though Marsha deals almost daily with those who would steal Jesus, her experience is witness to resurrection.

You have your stories, too. I've heard some of them.

I met recently with a man who grew up in fundamentalism and has now rejected both the church and faith in God. He understandably expressed his bitterness; he wanted nothing to do with those bigoted, harsh, hypocritical Christians. He was angry and damaged.

But I saw tenderness and hope cross his face as he sat in my office and wept. "There's something about Jesus that just won't die," he said, "just won't leave me alone. And, strangely, it's Jesus who helps me get through things." This young man may consider himself an atheist, but he has a resurrection story to tell, a story of a Jesus who refuses to be stolen by those who would distort his love.

In a study curriculum entitled *We Are an Easter People,* the authors ask:

> After Easter happened… what tangible evidence was there that anything had occurred? The only visible sign was a new religious community – a bunch of ordinary human beings… And yet, the first-century world quickly began to sense something re-markable was happening within [them]. A strange spirit was at work… a spirit which empowered them to face and to beat all the things which normally defeat us human beings in life.
>
> Somehow this little community had… a power which turned strangers from threats into gifts; wounded people into healers; self-centered folks into servants of others; victims into human beings who could live victoriously… (Carr, 47)

As we follow Jesus and invite him to stay with us and guide us, Christ lives, even when it appears that "they" have stolen Jesus yet again. When we, too, experience that intimate encounter, when Jesus comes to us, calls us by name, and stands beside us through it all, Christ Jesus is risen and here.

As we emerge from our own places of death, Jesus lives. When hope dawns, Jesus lives. When justice prevails, Jesus lives. When love empowers us to change, to love, to forgive, Jesus lives!

May our lives bear witness that Jesus is not stolen – then or now – but is risen!

12

BULLIES, BLOWS, AND BLESSINGS

From 1 Peter 3:13-22 (adapted)

Now who will harm you if you are eager to do what is good? But even if you do suffer for doing what is right, you are blessed. Do not fear what they fear, and do not be intimidated, but in your hearts sanctify Christ. Always be ready to make your defense to anyone who demands from you an accounting for the hope that is in you; yet do it with gentleness and reverence. Keep your conscience clear, so that, when you are maligned, those who abuse you for your good conduct may be put to shame. For it is better to suffer for doing good than to suffer for doing evil. For Christ also suffered for sins once for all, the righteous for the unrighteous, in order to bring you to God.

⁓

THE WRITER OF our epistle lesson for today asks this question: "Now who will harm you if you are eager to do what is good?"

Would anyone care to answer that for us? Given the text that follows, I wonder if this question was rhetorical. We *know* that it isn't always the shady characters who suffer; and we know that good motives or right actions don't exempt us from being harmed – from suffering.

If we consider only the widespread sufferings of the past year

[2010], we remember a devastating litany of pain, grief, fear, and abuse: the tsunami in Japan; suicides of gay teens and young adults who had experienced bullying in our schools; systematic rape condoned by governments; devastating tornados and hurricanes of unimaginable magnitude. And we could continue.

The writer of this epistle called 1 Peter speaks of a certain sort of suffering: suffering that is connected to faith and religious practice. You see, many of those of whom the writer speaks were called "transient strangers" and "resident aliens". Perhaps some were traveling merchants or refugees. Literally, they were day laborers without hope of permanent work. They spoke other languages, wore different clothing, and were treated with resentment, slander, and suspicion.

And they suffered. Suffering is mentioned over twenty times in the short book of 1 Peter. It was clearly written for real people facing real crises. They were being insulted and slandered because they were followers of Jesus – literally, because of the "name of Christ", one who was considered a crucified criminal.

We may think of "suffering for our faith" as something from long ago or far away. After all, we don't usually suffer persecution or even ridicule for getting up on Sunday mornings and going to church. Jails aren't full of people who don't smoke or drink or swear because of their faith. Hymn-singing isn't high on the list as a target for hate crimes or political persecution. We aren't punished for charitable acts – soup kitchens may even garner favor, as they save the government some money. And, at least in most Western countries, people aren't punished or even socially excluded for claiming to follow Jesus, to be Christian.

Does this text apply to us? Or do we only know about suffering "for our faith" from the pages of the scriptures or of history? Does suffering like this only occur in countries that oppress anyone who is different or who resists control?

In 2011, as reported in the *New York Times* (Goodstein), more than a hundred Catholic nuns from over twenty congregations wrote a letter to the Vatican protesting the threatened excommunication of the Reverend Roy Bourgeois, a priest who publicly speaks for the ordination of women and actually participated in ordaining a woman to the priesthood. Bourgeois was given thirty days to recant his public statements and deny his convictions or be excommunicated. He responded that he would not, he could not, do so.

Just last week, a member of the United States Congress actually rolled his eyes when a colleague of the opposite party spoke about her commitment to healthcare reform. She dared to express clearly her ethical position: that everyone has the right to medical attention and to be treated as a person of value, as they are in God's eyes. And he rolled his eyes and smirked. He ridiculed her passion for justice and equality.

And in these past months here in Atlanta, we have seen that people who express their faith by offering sanctuary and radical hospitality to those who seek economic refuge in our country are subject to punishment and suffering for taking such action.

Perhaps suffering for one's faith still goes on. And, therefore, we ask: How do we cope or continue to live in faith rather than fear? How does God respond with us or for us?

Theologian Dorothee Soelle makes this hard but truthful assertion: that "the Christian faith relates to suffering not merely as remover or consoler." (Soelle, *Suffering*, 155) In other words, God doesn't simply remove our pain or just say "There, there" with dismissive consolation. That isn't usually how it works. As we know, there is more to do, to learn, to accomplish, in and through suffering.

I just read a Facebook conversation in which the writer spoke of the deep faith struggle in which she was engaged because of the suffering of those who do good. She writes: "It's the one issue that

OUT ON A LIMB

really questions my faith. How can God permit such suffering?"

We don't want it to be so. We know life isn't fair, but this just isn't right! How do we manage? How do we live alongside our own suffering and that of others, especially when suffering is brought on by goodness or courageous action for what is right?

There are, of course, a number of typical human responses. We could respond by being the victim, by feeling self-pity and taking up residence there, licking our wounds. We could retaliate, hit back, pass the abuse on to someone else. We could be destroyed by it, just give up. We could blame God, as Job's friends suggested – curse God and die – assuming that God could and should relieve such suffering, or all suffering. We could be shamed or frightened into stopping whatever seems to bring the negative response. We could confront those who are causing the suffering, knowing as we do that bullies often respond by escalating the bullying behavior.

Our text offers us guidance, I believe, as we grapple with this sort of suffering in the world. First, it offers us comfort, but not the "there, there" sort. If we are suffering, if we experience ridicule or exclusion, if we are misunderstood because of how we live our lives, we are assured that we are not alone in our suffering. Jesus has suffered for the same sort of action, and his suffering made a statement that still rocks the world.

The words of Psalm 66 don't sugar-coat what human beings must sometimes endure, but they do tell us that suffering can bring us to a different place:

> You, O God, have tested us; you have tried us as silver is tried.
> You brought us into the net; you laid burdens on our backs;
> you let people ride over our heads; we went through fire and
>   through water;
> yet you have brought us out to a spacious place.

I love that! A spacious place, open, free, and grace-filled.

The second offering of our text is implicit: the challenge to follow Jesus. Emulating the ethics and actions of Jesus is the sort of faith-in-action for which we will surely suffer. It's the willingness to challenge the church, our families, and even governments when the ways of love, justice, kindness, and dignity are disregarded. Is our faith showing enough for people to notice? Does it insist on the values of justice and peace in a way that disturbs the comfort of those who are invested in maintaining the status quo?

We put them on alert when we insist that all of us are God's beloved, when we want to give those on whom our world has given up an extra break or the dignity of higher expectations, when we upset the structures of haves and have-nots, when we speak up for justice, and when we dare to connect justice for all with the name of Jesus.

Third, our text calls us to examine our own behaviors that cause suffering for others. Sometimes, suffering is even perpetrated against those in the church *by* those in the church. With betrayal of trust, gossip (which is rarely harmless or intended for good, even in the context of a prayer), and grumbling against those we say we love, we inflict suffering. Or perhaps we direct our painful words or judgments towards those who express their faith differently, those of other religions who worship or name God in different ways.

As Jesus, Gandhi, Martin Luther King, Simone Weil, and others have taught us, the only salvation in this despair is to go on loving. Will the way we practice our faith in times of suffering lead us to become "better people or bitter people"? Will we head toward "breakdown or breakthrough"? How can we keep from letting what happens to us "deform us or destroy us"? (McLaren, 14) The only salvation for us in this despair is to go on loving. This does not equate to continuing to take abuse. Rather, it means speaking the truth, even if it's from a distance, and refraining from retaliation.

The writer of 1 Peter calls us to be ready to give an account of the faith that we have in us, to speak to what serves the values of love and justice, to speak honestly of what we know, in both personal and public realms.

To follow in the way of love, we must keep our consciences clear. Take the high road. Refuse to hurl insult for insult. We must not give in to fear. Fear that would make us think twice about our justice-seeking action is all around us: from the latest terror alert to fearmongering debates about healthcare or the safety of our borders.

And, as those who find our model in Jesus, we can remember the sufferings of Christ. Not just to know that he understands. Rather, to know that Jesus suffered because he refused to stop valuing those on the margins. He wouldn't abandon his insistence on equality or give up his association with those some considered unclean. He kept on. And because he did, he suffered.

As Dorothee Soelle and Simone Weil remind us:

The only salvation for a person in this despair is to go on loving "in the void," a love for God that is no longer reactive, in answer to experienced happiness – the gratitude of a child – but instead an act that goes beyond all that has been experienced. (Soelle, *Suffering*, 156)

"The soul has to go on loving in the emptiness. Then, one day, God will come to… this soul." (Weil, cited in Soelle, *Suffering*, 156)

So, when we do the right thing and we are treated badly because of it – or in spite of it – what do we do? We choose to go on loving. And to continue to do what God calls us to do. To live with courage and hope even when we have no control over the actions of others.

As we suffer, as we stand with those who suffer, God will come to us with clarity, with more love to give, with insight, and with character.

13

SPIRITUAL HOUSE

1 Peter 2:2-10

Like newborn infants, long for the pure, spiritual milk, so that by it you may grow into salvation – if indeed you have tasted that the Lord is good. Come to Jesus, a living stone, rejected by mortals yet chosen and precious in God's sight, and like living stones, let yourselves be built into a spiritual house, to be a holy priesthood, to offer spiritual sacrifices acceptable to God through Jesus Christ.

For it stands in scripture: "See, I am laying in Zion a stone, a cornerstone chosen and precious." "The stone that the builders rejected has become the very head of the corner." You are a holy nation, God's own people, in order that you may proclaim the mighty acts of the one who called you out of darkness into marvelous light. Once you were not a people, but now you are God's people; once you had not received mercy, but now you have received mercy.

సౌ

LIKE LIVING STONES, let yourselves be built into a spiritual house.

Houses: where we live, are at home, free to be ourselves. Ideally, houses offer safety and shelter, a place of belonging, comfort, and nurture.

This poetic text offers us beautiful images of home in the community of Christ. It calls and invites us to become a spiritual house. The church is to be a *spiritual house,* not just a social and supportive community. Rather, we are to function like Christ – to be living stones that build this spiritual dwelling, a people whose presence is holy and loving.

The people to whom this letter was written understood the temple as the dwelling place of God. Solomon's temple was filled with the "glory" of God. This was the spiritual house where the presence of God was known, the very stones animated with the breath of God. The temple theology was clear: God lived there. Through worship in the temple, including singing songs and offering gifts, God's people remembered who they were and who Yahweh was to them.

But the temple – God's dwelling place – had been destroyed. The people of God were without home and without a spiritual house, without a place of belonging and without a house of God.

The writer offers us the richness of appropriating the word "house" as both "household", a place of acceptance and belonging, and as "temple", the dwelling place of God.

Peter invited his readers to keep coming to Jesus and to allow *themselves* to be built into a spiritual temple, join in the new covenant written on human hearts. To be both household/family and temple – a place of God's indwelling and of extravagant welcome.

The readers of 1 Peter don't need to depend on structures or formulations for a spiritual home; they can actually *be* the place of God's dwelling and offer that sense of home for others who are homeless.

Christ is the cornerstone of the soon-to-be-built spiritual house. The living stone, that is, a stone that has been broken and prepared for construction.

But houses aren't built of cornerstones alone. The spirit of God is not – could not be – contained in Christ alone. Rather, those to whom the text is written, and all who come after, were also to become living stones, and to let themselves be built into a spiritual house.

They – we – are to follow the One who is the Living Stone: not just believing the right things about Jesus, but cultivating that living relationship so that we're of the same substance – Living Stone to living stone. This is the cornerstone of the church: the Risen Christ alive in us. And as living stones, we, like Jesus, are dwelling places of God. The homeless were to become a home, a household, a family, a temple.

I've had the privilege of working with people who are experiencing homelessness. Part of that work was to help folks find affordable housing. I got to know a man called Charlie. Charlie had come a long way from his down-and-out days: he got a job, even got clean and mostly sober. But it was the oddest thing: Charlie refused to take an apartment.

I visited Charlie and tried to reason with him, to cajole him into safer accommodation. But I discovered the reason for Charlie's reluctance on a visit to his plywood home under a bridge. Charlie and about fifteen others lived there, sharing food that they bought or had been given, telling stories around a fire that was the center of their camp, and generally looking out for each other's safety. The stunning truth became clear: they shared a home. It was a spiritual house of sorts, where all were welcomed and cared for. Charlie had a lot to lose by leaving, and he wouldn't hear of it.

He had no building – no walls to contain anything. But Love was there, and mercy and compassion. Kindness and, yes, even hope. Charlie had a home that meant something to him, and he couldn't bear to face the loneliness of an apartment without the warmth that he found underneath the bridge.

> Come to him, a living stone, rejected by mortals yet chosen
> and precious in God's sight, and like living stones,
> let yourselves be built into a spiritual house. (1 Peter 2:4-5)

Spiritual houses are alive with meaning and ritual. Before the destruction of the Jerusalem temple, they had a place for ritual sacrifice, a defining part of their identity. But Peter suggests that they can now offer *spiritual* sacrifice: offering themselves as home, living lives of service, remaining in the light of love.

When I was teaching high school, I taught a number of students who lived at a local children's home. Most had been legally removed from their homes because of parental neglect or abuse. I joined the children in one of the cottages for dinner from time to time and quickly realized why some children who lived in "normal" homes thought they might like to live there. It was truly a spiritual house: a place of embrace for those discarded – with abundant hugs, talk of God, listening ears, and family rituals that offered security, peace, and meaning. The children themselves were being built into spiritual houses.

Are you at home with God? Is God building you – and us together – into a house in which others can also find home?

Perhaps you've left home – the home of faith itself or the home of spiritual community. Sometimes, as we grow and seek, we leave home. Don't we? At least for a while. Away from home, we may rediscover God or our need for God or for each other.

Maybe you have been gone from home too long. Are you ready to come home?

That gentle old gospel hymn invites us:

Softly and tenderly Jesus is calling.
All who are weary come home.
Calling, [Beloved], come home. (Thompson)

We're invited to come home and to be home – not alone, but together. Living stones joined to the corner.

And always, as we feel at home, we are called to remember those who have no home and to offer the shelter and nurture of the home that we are becoming. Surely, we must take the context to heart: those who follow Jesus are to become the house for those who are aliens and strangers and suffering ones. Become sanctuary.

We can be home and family for each other and for all who long for home. We don't need to wonder where God is; we can be the dwelling place of God here and now.

May we truly be that house – not just a façade, but a strong structure – from the depths of our souls to the character of our lives and relationships, that we might indeed be all that God is building us to be.

14

THE EUNUCH'S CHILDREN
Pride Sunday

Acts 8:26-39

Then an angel of the Lord said to Philip, "Get up and go toward the south to the road that goes down from Jerusalem to Gaza." (This is a wilderness road.) So he got up and went. Now there was an Ethiopian eunuch, a court official of Candace, queen of the Ethiopians, in charge of her entire treasury. He had come to Jerusalem to worship and was returning home; seated in his chariot, he was reading the prophet Isaiah. Then the Spirit said to Philip, "Go over to this chariot and join it." So Philip ran up to it and heard him reading the prophet Isaiah. He asked, "Do you understand what you are reading?" He replied, "How can I, unless someone guides me?" And he invited Philip to get in and sit beside him. Now the passage of the scripture that he was reading was this: "Like a sheep he was led to the slaughter, and like a lamb silent before its shearer, so he does not open his mouth. In his humiliation justice was denied him. Who can describe his generation? For his life is taken away from the earth." The eunuch asked Philip, "About whom, may I ask you, does the prophet say this, about himself or about someone else?"

Then Philip began to speak, and starting with this scripture, he proclaimed to him the good news about Jesus. As they were going along the road, they came to some water; and the eunuch said, "Look, here is water! What is to prevent me from being baptized?" He commanded the chariot to stop, and both of them, Philip and the eunuch, went down into the water, and Philip baptized him. When they came up out of the water, the Spirit of the Lord snatched Philip away; the eunuch saw him no more, and went on his way rejoicing.

⁊

QUAKER THEOLOGIAN Parker Palmer has written:

> People who plant the seeds of movements make a critical decision: they decide to live "divided no more." They decide no longer to act on the outside in a way that contradicts some truth about themselves that they hold deeply on the inside. They decide to claim their authentic selfhood and act it out, and their decisions ripple out to transform the society in which they live. (Palmer, 32)

Lesbian, gay, bisexual, and transgender people have much to celebrate during this year's Pride festivals [2009], in this fortieth anniversary of the Stonewall riots of 1969. We celebrate legal marriage and civil partnerships in a growing number of nations, election of gay and women bishops in more and more denominations, increasing safety in work environments, and unprecedented acceptance by our families. Around the world, brave activists are challenging laws and practices that violate human rights, with demands for change. But we still have work to do.

We still have dreams to dream and risks to take so that all may be equal in the law and in the church, in our families and through our faith. As lesbian, gay, bisexual, and transgender people of faith and those who stand with us, our work takes on yet another dimension. We dare to confront the bastion of sexual denial. You know what it is, right? The church.

The church has, blatantly or subtly, denied the goodness of human sexuality for much of our history. But we raise our voices and our lives in celebration of, in our experience of, the unity of sexuality and spirituality – of sex and spirit – spoken in the same breath and celebrated as part of the beauty in human life.

We are saying, when we march in Pride parades under the

banners of churches, that in this body is both queer sexuality and a spirit that is in deep communion with God, that we are living *divided no more*.

As Christians who dare to speak of sex and Spirit, we hold this dangerous tension between the mystery of and our passion for God and the mystery of and our passion for another. We believe that both – together – are integral parts of what it means to be fully human and created in the image of God.

Historically, the church has made it clear: Spirit is more holy than body. In fact, we hear phrases like "the desires of the flesh" and are told that this desire, presumably sexual in nature, keeps us from knowing and serving God.

The book of Genesis tells the story of the serpent, Eve and Adam. It says that Adam and Eve disobeyed by eating the forbidden fruit. Isn't it interesting that we put terms like that around sex, calling it "forbidden fruit"?

The punishments that ensued were all about sex, body, and gender: shame in nakedness, pain in childbirth, and the hierarchy of man over woman. No wonder the church has taken a while to come back to the goodness of creation!

But I don't think this story describes God's intention for humankind. Rather, I think it describes just how fragmented we human beings are when we hide our nakedness, our body-selves, from each other and even from God. Did you notice that when God came around, they covered themselves?

Sexual and spiritual fragmentation has been the state of the church. If it's about God, we can't say too much about sexual pleasure. And if we're talking about sex, we have a shadow of fear that God can't be in it and probably wouldn't approve of our sex-talk.

Here is a clear example of how fragmented we are as people

of faith. We're perfectly willing to say, as the church has said for centuries, that Jesus was fully human. But just watch how uncomfortable people, including us, become at the suggestion that Jesus may have been a sexual being: that he even had sexual feelings, much less that he may have related sexually with another. That's revealing, isn't it, of how we feel about speaking of sex and God in the same breath. It's somehow unholy!

I remember my first Pride parade years ago in the city of Atlanta, Georgia. We marched past church after church. Red-faced evangelicals shook bibles in our faces and shouted curses (literally) and quoted scripture out of context. But we represented the church, too.

I pondered for a long time, asking what stirs all that hatred and anger. Why are lesbian, gay, bisexual, and transgender people of faith such an affront to much of the church?

I believe that our offense is this: We dare to say that we were created for intimacy with God and another, that we long for God as the deer longs for water and a desire for another runs deep into our soul. We proclaim with our very beings that desire, longing, passion is innate to being human *and is good*. We dare to say, with audacious lives, that sex may even be a place of encounter with God, an intimate window to the mystery of ultimate holiness.

Our quest for marriage equality has made our offense more visible. Our marriages, especially when they are celebrated in our places of worship, state clearly our unwillingness to live divided lives. We make no attempt to deny that sexuality and spirituality, sex and spirit, come together in our marriages. We can't camouflage it like straight people can. For LGBT folks, it's not entangled in the mythology of family or in the fairytale world of the knight and the princess.

Now we know that gay and lesbian relationships are

multi-dimensional; they aren't just about sex. But for many observers, some of the media, and the religious right, our relationships aren't real relationships, they're about sex. And here we are – flaunting it in God's house.

I for one think that's a good thing.

You see, we're saying it out loud: this sex-is-bad-spirit-is-good theology is just plain wrong. It isn't godly; it was never the intention for any of us – gay or straight – to live divided. We're saying that knowing and being known is beautiful and good and teaches us about God. We dare to say that desire is the spark, that passion is life-giving, that we experience intimacy with God and sexual intimacy, even at the same time.

Our world needs to be healed from this spiritual brokenness. The church needs to be healed from spiritual brokenness. We've divided ourselves in the name of God for way, way too long. And, it doesn't really matter if you're gay or straight; the message is for all.

I love this story of Philip and the Ethiopian eunuch. Philip, a disciple of Jesus, had a conversation with a eunuch, that is, a man who was some sort of sexual minority. In first-century writings, the term *eunuch* can refer to a variety of sexual or gender minorities, in addition to the familiar reference to castrated males.

The eunuch, according to Jewish understanding, did not have the religious status of a man who was a patriarch, a father. The writers of the Hebrew Bible compare him to a dry tree. He would have no descendants; he was the end of the line and a spiritual curse, really.

Philip told this eunuch the story of how God's love is known in Jesus, how Jesus loved and healed and brought God to all, especially to those who were excluded. Then the eunuch, sexual outsider that he was, asked a courageous question. "Here is water," he said. "What is to prevent me from being baptized?"

The eunuch seems to shout at us from the pages of scripture: "Wait! That Genesis saga isn't the whole story. I can be one whose sexuality defines him and a follower of Christ!"

My friends, they thought he had no descendants. But, in a profound spiritual way, God's LGBT people and those who are on the margins with us are the eunuch's descendants. We have asked the question, too: "What is to prevent us from being baptized, from having our gay, lesbian, trans, straight and out bodies marked as God's own?"

Here is the table. What is to keep us from being fed? *Here is the pulpit.* What is to prevent us from telling our stories about how God is real in our lives? *Here is the blessing of marriage.* What is to prevent us from receiving it? Let's go even further: *Here is our bedroom.* What is to prevent us from encountering God in sacred, joyful, delightful sex?

We are the eunuch's descendants, queer people who love God and seek God's blessing. And I believe that we know a profound secret that the world longs to know. Our secret is this: in the light of God's love, we can be made whole. We don't have to live divided anymore; gay, straight, trans – none of us have to be divided anymore. We don't have to confine parts of ourselves to the shadow places of life, whispering in secret, covering our nakedness. God can heal our separation of body and soul, of sexuality and spirituality, of sex and spirit. We can integrate and celebrate our passions and love God and another with holy fire and blessing.

This, my friends, is a gift that same-gender-loving people bring to the church.

May we receive God's blessing that heals our own divisions, so that we can offer this message of hope with courage and joy.

15

BEYOND WOMEN AND MEN

This sermon, like the last, "The Eunuch's Children," is based on the eighth chapter of Acts (see p112). It was part of a series on the distinctive characteristics of Decatur United Church of Christ, Decatur, Georgia, where I served as Senior Minister from 2010 to 2014. This sermon moves on from the issue of sexuality and the church, to look at the text's implications regarding gender.

The distinctive characteristic that serves as the basis for this sermon is: We realize that social mores, stereotypes, and misinterpretations of scripture have limited the spirituality, creativity, and social acceptance of those who don't comply with binary gender norms; and we want to make a difference by exploring issues of gender and gender expression. Further, we realize that this is a theological issue as well as a social issue.

ᴄ⁄ꜱ

OUR CONSTANT SUNDAY morning purpose is to experience the Spirit's transforming ways; to encounter the living God who inspires, comforts, challenges, and loves us beyond measure.

This morning, as we continue to explore the distinctive identity of our congregation, we'll consider issues of gender and gender expression. Like each of our distinctive characteristics, this one could be the basis of a series of classes all its own. Gender is a topic that rarely gets mentioned, at least in a direct and intentional way, in worship. And yet, it's vitally important to how we minister to one another and how we become a fully welcoming congregation. It's important to all of us, to each of us, as we grow in our relationship with God and each other.

So, I invite us to approach prayerfully this morning. We tread on the holy ground of God's diverse creation.

I'm going to begin addressing today's statement by telling you that I had a relatively content and comfortable childhood. I know this sounds like a statement better suited to a therapist's office than to a pulpit, but it has much to do with our priority for being concerned – both socially and theologically – about gender issues.

Yes, it's true. I had loving parents, a wonderful church, a mother who sewed all my clothing with love and skill, an attentive father who taught me to appreciate art and design, a piano teacher I adored. I had plenty of open space in which to play baseball, a great bicycle, and a few friends with whom to share it all. And my parents, somewhat shockingly for Southern Baptist Republicans, didn't stifle my hopes and dreams or regulate my activities according to my gender.

But I also had two profound disappointments. Remembering them – even now – brings that pain back. The first one strikes me as a bit funny now, but I was shocked and dismayed at the time. I was an avid baseball player as a kid, and I remember the day I was told that women weren't allowed to play professional baseball. I had never dreamt of such a ridiculous prohibition!

My second disappointment was similar. I eventually realized that the church I loved and wanted to give my life to had only two jobs for me. I could choose to work with children, or I could be a missionary in some far-off country, hidden away. Being a woman in ministry in the open was not an option.

We all know the expectations and assignments that come with gender. It's either pink or blue. Trucks or dolls. Lace or Levis. Toughness or tears. Soft or sensible. Boy or girl. One or the other. And we think it's determined when the doctor makes the pronouncement: "It's a girl!" As far back as any of us can remember, it's either/or: son or daughter, man or woman, male or female, ladies or gentlemen.

This is what Christian author Virginia Mollenkott calls the "binary gender construct." *Binary*, of course, means two; *construct* means that we created it; we made it up. (Mollenkott, 9)

What *is* gender anyway? Is it just about our bodies, about hormones and hips? Hormones, for sure, but also chromosomes and brain structure and the predictable (and sometimes unpredictable) physiology.

In her book *Omnigender: a Trans-Religious Approach*, Mollenkott reveals a fact about gender and the 1996 Olympic Games that were held here in Atlanta, Georgia. It seems that some women – women who had given birth to children, thereby being physiologically female – were not allowed to participate in women's athletic events because chromosomally they were not women. (Mollenkott, 47)

Clearly, this indicates that multiple factors contribute to one's gender assignment, and that two of those factors – physiology and chromosome structure – can send mixed signals.

Our perceived gender dictates how we're conditioned, the behaviors and gender roles that we're expected to follow. Taking their cues from our bodies, our parents and teachers shaped us in the prevailing gender molds: *Boys don't cry! Be ladylike – cross your legs.*

Our culture schools us to accept that men are better at some jobs and women at others; that women are – or certainly should be – more tender and nurturing, men more rational and protective.

Brain Sex is the title of a book written by two British physicians. The writers clearly and scientifically explain the exact differences in the structure of typical male brains and typical female brains. They seem to subscribe to every gender stereotype that has led to centuries of shaming women and elevating men. That is, until they begin to talk about those who have a typical male brain in a "female" body – or a typical female brain in a "male" body – or some sort of hybrid brain structure that doesn't conform to the norm. (Moir and Jessel, 24-25) And, then, of course, we must consider that the characteristics of the male brain have served as something of a baseline for normalcy, with the resulting prejudices and definitions of superiority.

Gender, my friends, is not so clear as male and female. And it's not just about our bodies. Those who have something about them that crosses a gender boundary – gender transgressors, or "gender outlaws," a term that author Kate Bornstein coins – embody physical, mental, and emotional characteristics that defy our gender expectations. I believe that this includes many of us – many more than we even imagine.

What in the world – you might be wondering – does any of this have to do with God, or with our church? I believe it has much to do with God and with the church's mission in the world.

Now we know that the Bible was written with a patriarchal world-view. And the Bible – at least on the surface – presents two genders: one strong, in the image of the Holy God, the other weak in body and soul. But, according to the first chapter of Genesis: "God created humankind in God's own image, in the image of God, male and female God created them." (Genesis 1:27)

The Bible also has some hidden exceptions to these patriarchal stereotypes, rules, and taboos: Deborah, Hagar, Ruth, David, Jonathan, Potiphar, Shiphrah and Puah, Esther. Strong, in-charge women and sensitive, soft men.

The Bible also speaks of other gender-crossing men, using the term *eunuch*. Here's a passage from Deuteronomy that just about sums it up:

> The one whose testicles are crushed or whose male member is cut off [one meaning of eunuch] shall not enter the assembly of the Lord. (Deuteronomy 23:1)

Many scholars contend that the term *eunuch* was also used for those who don't quite fit the clear male/female delineation. For a variety of reasons, eunuchs don't belong to their original or apparent gender.

Israel was surrounded by civilizations in which eunuchs were exploited, used as slaves or as temple servants. In order to be differentiated and separate from other religious cultures, Israel excluded eunuchs from worship. Only "real" men were invited to the inner court of the temple.

However, the prophet Isaiah envisions that the realm of God's new covenant will overturn this exclusion:

> Do not let the eunuch say, "I am just a dry tree."
> For thus says Yahweh: "To the eunuchs who keep my Sabbaths,
> who choose the things that please me and hold fast my covenant,
> I will give in my house and within my walls a monument
> and a name better than sons and daughters;
> I will give them an everlasting name which shall not be cut off."
> (Isaiah 56:3c-5)

The criteria for pleasing God are the choices one makes and the content of one's character, rather than conforming to gender laws.

In the story of Philip and the Ethiopian eunuch, Philip, a disciple of Jesus, had a conversation with a eunuch. The eunuch – who had come to Jerusalem to worship – undoubtedly knew his disqualification and had assuredly experienced that exclusion.

Did you notice the detail, though? The eunuch was reading the scriptures – but you notice he wasn't reading Genesis. No – he was reading Isaiah, the prophet who envisioned the embrace of eunuchs in the covenant community.

Philip told him the story of how God's love is known in Jesus, how Jesus loved and healed and brought God to all, especially to those who were excluded. He explained that Jesus even taught about eunuchs, saying that some were born that way, others were made, and some chose to be eunuchs. Jesus urged people to accept this!

Then the eunuch – sexual outsider that he was – asked a courageous question: *Here is water*, he said. *What is to prevent me from being baptized?* He claimed his desire to be connected with the people of God, regardless of his designation as a sexual outsider.

As Jesus knew millennia ago, not everyone is born male or female. In fact, indeterminate or mixed-genital gender is much more common than most of us realize.

Jesus said that God also created those who are born as eunuchs and belong in neither of the two categories of male or female. Maintaining the notion that human beings all fall unequivocally into two genders is simply made up. It's denying scientific fact and the witness of the Bible – in spite of itself!

Are you free from gender-determined restrictions on your behavior or dress or vocation? Are you free to wear your hair as you please? To like what you like and feel what you feel – without constraint from either inside or outside that says men don't do that or feel that way, women don't say those words or go to those sorts of places?

Of course, this is about sexuality – but it's really about gender. This issue spans the spectrum of sexual orientation. Why do you think, gentlemen, that you may have been called "sissies" or been given toy trucks instead of dolls? It's because we must be one or the other – our culture insists!

But *in Christ there is no Jew or Greek, no male or female.* (Galatians 3:28) Take it in. Can you feel the release, the freedom?

Some of us, I dare to speculate, enjoy being strong; we cry during tender moments at the movies; we like wearing cargo trousers... and evening gowns... and tuxedos. We enjoy both rational discussion and emotionally probing conversation. We are ready competitors on athletic fields and also think our eyes look much better with a bit of mascara. We express ourselves best in poetry, are secretly scared of spiders, love caring for babies, and – dare I say this one? – enjoy going to the indoor shooting range.

Who am I if all those characteristics belong to me? (Which they do.) Am I simply an outsider who doesn't belong or must hide or change or pretend in order to find a place in the church and the world?

God has great hope and design for us. It is the desire of the heart of God that each of us will be and become all we can be. Some of us – most of us, perhaps – experience cultural or religious constraints that keep us from being our authentic, true, full selves: those rules and taboos and expectations about gender. We're stopped or silenced or shamed or punished; we're considered less than those made in God's image if we don't comply with and conform to those expectations.

I challenge all of us: Each day, set yourself free! Acknowledge all the maleness, femaleness, and otherness in yourself and give thanks to the One who created every aspect of you with holy intention.

As the people of God in this place, we're called to offer radical hospitality and generous welcome; to honour others – all others – as those created in the image of God. Hospitality means letting all gender boundary-crossers know that they are welcome without shame or fear.

Hospitality means that we openly and clearly welcome transgender folk and that we say that out loud! If we don't say the names of the other, they won't know they're included. Saying everyone is welcome simply isn't enough, nor the whole story.

And we're invited to know God more deeply through the spectrum of gender. That means that we look around us – all around us – to see the faces of God. We look at God's creation to discover who God is and, unless we consider the diversity of creation, including the full spectrum of genders, we're missing part of God's image.

A hymn that many inclusive churches sing says this:

Our God is not a woman; our God is not a man –
Our God is both and neither; our God is I who am. (Bernier)

Both and neither. A transgender God? An intersexed God? Yes!

In all creation, God crosses boundaries and barriers that we humans keep trying to establish.

This is worship. It's God-honoring to recognize God in all her strength, in all his beauty, in various expressions of our genders in the Trans-trinity. God as three, Christian doctrine says: male, female, neuter.

Not so humbly, I consider myself something of an expert at inclusive language in the church. I've been practicing and teaching it, both practically and theologically, for over twenty-five years.

But my understanding was expanded recently, when a worship leader further inclusified a lyric to a song. The original says this: "Brother/Sister, let me love you; let me be as Christ to you." (Gillard)

But our brilliant liturgist changed it to read: "Every sibling, let me love you..." (Reay)

This change offers a deeper inclusivity – more than brothers and sisters. *Every* gender is our kin.

Perhaps we could stop having boxes to tick to indicate gender. Or we could speak of tenors and basses, rather than men and women in the choir. This is how we build authentic community and offer life. We touch people as children of God, as those who embody Christ just as we do. And we see the face of God more deeply.

May it be so.

ASCENSION

16

WHERE *SHOULD* WE LOOK?

Acts 1:1-11

So when they had come together, they asked him, "Lord, is this the time when you will restore the kingdom to Israel?" He replied, "It is not for you to know the times or periods that God has set by his Divine authority. But you will receive power when the Holy Spirit has come upon you; and you will be my witnesses in Jerusalem, in all Judea and Samaria, and to the ends of the earth."

When he had said this, as they were watching, he was lifted up, and a cloud took him out of their sight. While he was going and they were gazing up toward heaven, suddenly two men in white robes stood by them. They said, "People of Galilee, why do you stand looking up toward heaven?"

℘

Today is Ascension Sunday; we consider the event of Jesus' ascension as recorded in the writings of Luke/Acts. This story connects Jesus to Elijah, who also ascended into heaven, as witnessed by Elisha, the prophet who followed his legacy.

Could the story of the Ascension of Jesus really have meaning for us today? Could it mean something other than "go up" into the sky?

Some historical Jesus researchers are quick to tell you that the
Ascension never actually happened. It is a story, they say, that the
church took from the Hebrew scriptures to connect Jesus to the
prophets. If you had been there with your video camera on that
day, they tell us, there would have been nothing to record, no feet
of Jesus getting ever smaller as they rose into the sky.

While I don't think we can summarily dismiss the possibility
of a physical ascension – after all levitation has been claimed for
yogis and other holy men and women – we may miss the point if
we focus strictly on geography and physics rather than the spiritual
implication and meaning of the story.

Disciples of Jesus had followed and observed his way of living
and moving. They had seen and heard amazing, challenging,
puzzling teaching and had been caught up in his God-rooted
political and social movement. And for the last forty-something
days, they had experienced Jesus in an incomprehensible way –
following his death, he had been with them. Embodied, somehow.
They continued to experience Emmanuel – God-with-us.

But – did you notice that whenever Jesus was in a mystical
place with God: in the garden, on the cross, walking on the water,
healing diseased bodies and minds, he was alone in it? His followers
were on the outside looking in.

But now – he's given them a promise: the promise of Spirit
and Power. That spiritual connection with God, that first-hand
co-existence, that baptism with and in the spirit – drenching with
the Spirit was to be theirs. Those Jesus experiences with God, that
intimate knowing, that oneness, the flow of power in and through
was to fall on them!

St. Augustine said that the ascension "let our hearts ascend with
Jesus." (Augustine, 1)

Ascension says something about Jesus, but today, I'd like to consider what the ascension began in Jesus' followers and how we can share in it.

About Jesus, Marcus Borg, professor, scholar and author, writes:

> Because the risen and ascended Jesus is "one with God," he (like God) can be experienced anywhere. Jesus is no longer restricted or confined to time and space, as he was during his historical lifetime. Rather, like the God whom he knew in his own experience, he continues to be known in the experience of his followers. (Borg, 97)

Jesus has gone before us and is available to us, from the very heart of God. The risen and ascended Christ takes a place as spiritual counselor, Wisdom Itself, spiritually present beyond the confines of time and physicality. Jesus is unleashed into the world – spiritually present in both realms – making evident that we, too, can live on a spiritual plane, in that meeting place where human and divine come together. This – ascension, living in a spiritual realm – is something all human beings are capable of.

Jesus' followers who experienced the ascension looked up into heaven. But those who joined them said that Jesus would "return" in the same way, that is, spiritually. Physically looking up into the sky wouldn't give them the Jesus experience, the power and guidance and God experience for which they longed.

But where should they, where should we, look to find the presence of the ascended God-with-us? Where might we find the Christ?

A hint: Where is your ascension place? Think about it. Where (not necessarily in a physical place) have you experienced the extraordinary, mystical, spiritual power and presence of God?

When I was a child, I devised a praying place: a plank across two limbs of a sturdy mimosa tree. There I gazed heavenward and inward. I felt the breeze and the warmth of the sun and communed deeply with the Jesus of my childhood. In adulthood, I have experienced profound spiritual, mystical connection in the depths of the ocean on many diving trips and have known the Wisdom of the ascended and available One in those beyond-explanation promptings that guide and bring timely insight. And, perhaps most movingly, I have encountered the ascended and ever-present Christ in men and women whose very survival depends on the breath of God: those without shelter, those in prison, those struggling with addictions.

Dan Brown's popular book *The Da Vinci Code* is based on the notion that Jesus and Mary Magdalene had a child and, therefore, a physical Jesus bloodline exists. A theory that is possible, if unlikely. But the news of the gospel is better than that – more astounding and with much farther-reaching implications: the church's story is that we are the Jesus Spirit-line!

Like Elijah before him, Jesus passes his spiritual power and connection, his spiritual essence, to all who open themselves to be joined with him. It is we who become the chalice, the biological container of the essence of God-with-us.

May today be an ascension event as we realize the words to the great Easter hymn:

"Made like Christ, like Christ we rise!" (Wesley, 233)

We rise into the presence, into the being of Christ, into the communion and power and being of God.

Why do you stand looking up into heaven? Look around. And within. Look to inner experience. And places of service. *Be* Christ in the world – and you, too, will ascend. Rely on the power and wisdom of God – open yourself to it – and you, too, will ascend to heights of wonder and wisdom and eternal love.

17

LEFT BEHIND

In this sermon we consider the same passage as in the last: Acts1:1-11 (see p129).

(see p129)

ↄ

I REMEMBER CLEARLY the day my son, Philip, graduated from high school. In many ways, he was a young man ready to meet the world. In others, he was a sweet, silly, curious boy – hardly ready for independence.

This is a milestone that each of us probably remembers – as academic passage, perhaps, but primarily as life passage. More than any other marker in American culture, this event signals and allows strides toward independence.

As parents, we see this passage for our children with mixed emotions; we may anticipate some of the mistakes that lie ahead, the lessons to be learned, the struggles that are sure to accompany the joys of growing up. Just as Philip's life and role in the family has changed since that day, so have mine and his dad's. And I know that's good.

As much as I may have still wanted to protect him and design plans for him, as much as I wanted him to have fifty-year-old judgment (mine, of course) rather than young-adult hormones; the tasks of living, working, and loving have become his.

I only need to remember a friend from my high school years to realize the dangers of not letting go – of holding on when it's time to release. Fran is three years older than I am and still lives with her mother. Seriously! And, in some ways, their roles haven't changed at all. I would venture to say that Fran hasn't fully become who she could have been if she had left home to make a life of her own.

The hazards are obvious enough: remaining overly dependent; deferring inappropriately in decision-making and priorities; limiting her relationships; keeping a tight circle; not building a life of her own; not exploring her own personhood in an independent way; never developing her own sense of personal power. And even that new and different adult–adult relationship with her mother never had a chance, really.

I wonder if Fran has ever "grown up."

Jesus is drawing to the close of his post-resurrection time on earth. You can imagine that his friends are experiencing fear and dread. Fear that it was all a dream; dread that he could leave them again. Jesus moves them through their fears with signs that he is real and present with them. He has taught and modeled. He has passed on his wisdom and showed them what's important: Prayer and the poor. Justice and liberation. Equity and hope. Trust and honor. The ways and will of the realm of God.

As they experience him one last time, he commissions them, declares them witnesses and promises that they will be clothed with power from on high.

In Acts, this is a powerful commission and promise:

But you will receive power when the Holy Spirit has come upon you; and you will be my witnesses in Jerusalem, in all Judea and Samaria, and to the ends of the earth. (Acts 1:8)

Then he blesses them, withdraws from them and ascends into heaven. Gone. Again.

The time had come for the church – yet unformed, still unsure of all that had happened with Jesus, perhaps doubting their own experience, but sure of what Jesus had done for them – it was time for those who had lived alongside this Jesus to begin to become the body of Christ in the world.

The gospel story – the story of the life of Jesus – has come to completion, and the story of the church has begun. The same writer, the author of the gospel of Luke, continues the story in the book of Acts.

The story unfolds in the life of the people of Yahweh: God was known to God's people in the exodus, in the Promised Land, in exile, in the scriptures – the law and prophets. Then some saw the story continue in the person of Jesus.

In something of the same way that a parent sends a graduating son or daughter into the world – fragile, bold, zealous, and timid – Jesus anoints this unsure, faltering, yet prepared and transformed people. God will be present in them and through them. Taught. Prepared as best he and they could.

Jesus passes to them an inheritance – a spiritual trust – and the power of Spirit to help it flourish and grow. He passes on his connection with God so that the world may know transforming love, so that the love and power can endure generation to generation. So that it can be relevant in each age and community.

In the same way that Fran's life and relationship with her mother were compromised because the letting go never happened, Jesus' remaining with them would have kept them – and us – from being the witnesses that we can be as fully empowered people of God.

In the power of his light, we might never let ours shine. In the healing of his touch, we might never allow ourselves to heal others. If he was feeding the hungry, we would stand in line to be fed rather than offering food to others.

I remember hearing an explanation of Jesus' ascension when I was a child. It went something like this: "Jesus had to leave or the Spirit couldn't come." I think that the person who said this meant that somehow Jesus and the Spirit couldn't occupy the same space – and in that concrete, definitive way, this is certainly an inadequate explanation.

But perhaps in another way, it is true.

If Jesus had somehow remained physically present, the disciples and we might not have been able to *receive* the power of the Spirit in the same way. They saw the Spirit of God in Jesus – and might have kept it there, not allowing themselves to become the bearers of that Spirit, the healers of the sick, those who feed the hungry, and offer reconciliation to those who are separated from each other and from God. They – we – might not have become people of prayer, preachers of the sacred worth of all people.

But Jesus does leave; he does promise them the Spirit. And the Word becomes flesh once again – in the church.

We experience Jesus and we, too, are commissioned as witnesses. It just follows, doesn't it? Out of our experience, we offer the touch of Christ to the world. We're *christed*, really. We *become* the body of God in our time. And we touch others and it continues.

Like those first followers, we're promised the Spirit – power from on high – and given a blessing. Similarly to how we offer our blessings to our children when they move to a more inde-pendent place in life – putting trust in them, assuring them of our support and friendship as adults, allowing them to grow up, confident that their experience and learning will take them where they need to go – so Jesus blesses his friends and us, putting trust in us, staying close, confident that our relationship with God will call us, empower us and inspire us to be faithful witnesses.

In Jesus' blessing *he calls us to grow up*, to move from childish dependence to friendship with God and to become vessels of the Spirit, witnesses, and lovers.

What passages do we need to make, as individuals and as a people? How do we need to grow up, to let go, to become? What are we grasping at, holding onto, that keeps us from being receptive to the Spirit's empowerment? What have we received from Jesus that we need in order to *be* Jesus in our world?

What a message – promised the Spirit and blessed so that we can grow up, so that we can become Christ in our time and our place.

So when they had come together, they asked him, "Lord, is this the time when you will restore the kingdom to Israel?" He replied, "… you will receive power when the Holy Spirit has come upon you; and you will be my witnesses in Jerusalem, in all Judea and Samaria, and to the ends of the earth."

When he had said this, as they were watching, he was lifted up, and a cloud took him out of their sight.

While he was going and they were gazing up toward heaven, suddenly two men in white robes stood by them. They said, "People of Galilee, why do you stand looking up toward heaven?" (Acts 1:1-11)

The Body of Christ is alive all around you and in you.

PENTECOST

18

SELAH

Ezekiel 37:1-10

The hand of God came upon me, and brought me out by the Spirit and set me down in the middle of a valley; it was full of bones. God led me all around them; there were very many lying in the valley, and they were very dry. Then the One who brought me there said to me, "Mortal, can these bones live?" I answered, "O God, you know." And again God said to me, "Prophesy to these bones, and say to them: O dry bones, hear the word of the Lord. Thus says the Lord God to these bones: I will cause breath to enter you, and you shall live. I will lay sinews on you, and will cause flesh to come upon you, and cover you with skin, and put breath in you, and you shall live; and you shall know that I am the Holy One." So I prophesied as I had been commanded; and as I prophesied, suddenly there was a noise, a rattling, and the bones came together, bone to its bone. I looked, and there were sinews on them, and flesh had come upon them, and skin had covered them; but there was no breath in them. Then God said to me, "Prophesy to the breath, prophesy, mortal, and say to the breath: Thus says the Lord God: Come from the four winds, O breath, and breathe upon these slain, that they may live." I prophesied as I was commanded, and the breath came into them, and they lived, and stood on their feet, a vast multitude.

John 20:19-23

When it was evening on that day, the first day of the week, and the doors of the house where the disciples had met were locked for fear of the Jews, Jesus came and stood among them and said, "Peace be with you." After he said this, he showed them his hands and his side. Then the disciples rejoiced when they saw the Lord. Jesus said to them again, "Peace be with you. As the Author of Life has sent me, so I send you." When he had said this, he breathed on them and said to them, "Receive the Holy Spirit."

ᚼ

IN 2005, *NEWSWEEK* magazine presented an extensive study on spirituality in America. Researchers interviewed religious people, including Christians, Jews, and Muslims; nominally religious people; and non-religious people from a variety of places around the United States, including cities, towns and remote villages. Interviewees were of all ages and levels of education. The writers presented their stunning findings: that most human beings have a deep spiritual longing. We want to have an *experience* of the transcendent, to be touched by, to connect with, to be in the presence of holiness. (Adler)

We, as Christians, would say that we all long for the *spirit*, the *ruach* – that beautiful Hebrew word that means breath, wind, or spirit. Part of the meaning of a spiritual life is that we breathe out our living-on-the-surface life and breathe in a deep, primal hope and contentment.

Ruach. Breathe in; breathe out.

Now, I don't normally tell jokes in sermons, but this one may offer us a helpful reminder. So, I'll make an exception this time. A further apology is needed to those who, like me, are blonde. I hope that we'll all look beyond any insult!

A blonde wearing earphones attached to an iPod entered a hair salon and asked for a haircut. The stylist kindly requested that she remove the earphones, which she good-naturedly declined to do. He cut around them as best he could, thinking it all quite weird. What could be so important for her to hear non-stop?

About a month later the client returned and the same exchange took place. The stylist was irritated, as this, of course, compromised his artistry. On the third round another month later, the stylist could stand it no longer; so, when the client sat in the chair, he didn't ask if she would remove them. He simply reached over and removed her earphones himself. Seconds later, his lovely blonde client keeled over – fell from the chair to the floor – out cold. Frantically, he picked up the earphones and listened to the repetitive message: "Breathe in; breathe out. Breathe in; breathe out…"

Sometimes – spiritually – I need those headphones! I need those headphones because I can be so task-oriented in both worship and living that I forget to take in the breath of Spirit. I go through days, waiting to exhale – holding my breath with anxiety and diligence – and miss the animating, liberating wind of the Spirit.

Our theme for this weekend together is *Selah,* that undefined, enigmatic term that occurs in the some of the Psalms. *Selah* may be an instruction for performers or worshipers, perhaps a musical term, calling for a cymbal crash or the singing of a refrain. Many scholars believe it could be a pause, signaling singers or the congregation to stop and wait.

Or, with some witty biblical speculators, we could go with the idea that *Selah* was an expletive that David used every time he broke a harp string.

Since the exact meaning of *Selah* is unknown, I guess we can pick our favorite definition. I quite like the call to stop and reflect, to ponder what we've just heard or seen or experienced.

Stop and listen! Be still and know. Consider the mystery. Find the wisdom. Take time to breathe it in. Breathe. The Spirit stirs in worship. Stop. Listen. Selah! Breathe in: ruach, ruach.

The story of Ezekiel's vision of dry bones in the valley is part of the prophet's dream sequence. He sees a valley full of dry bones.

The writer of Ezekiel composes beautiful poetry, in which God offers two reasons for this pile of bones: first, the enemies of the nation of Israel have overtaken them, plundering their cities and destroying their land. Israel, in its weakness and desolation, has suffered the insults of nations who have oppressed them.

But that's not all. God makes it clear that the people of Israel are not blameless. They may have been victimized, but they have also brought destruction on themselves. They participated in their own demise, killing others and worshiping that which is not God.

And so, in the dream, God asks the prophet: "Oh, mortal, can these bones live?" (Ezekiel 37:3) Duh – obvious answer! Bones are, well, dead. But Ezekiel, sensing that this might be a trick question, turns it right back to God. And God instructs Ezekiel to prophesy – preach – to the bones. (Now, there's a congregation!) So Ezekiel does, and you know what happens then.

In the words of the old traditional spiritual, "Dem Bones":

The foot bone connected to the ankle bone,
the ankle bone connected to the leg bone.
O hear the word of the Lord!

The bones connected – formed a body, a skeleton; but they were still not alive. All the "parts" were in the right place. Lined up and attached, sinews and flesh.

It's a bit like a worship service with every part plugged in where our tradition says it goes. Have you experienced worship like that? Perfectly constructed but dry and dusty. Like those dry bones, those who seek to experience God through worship need more than that.

But I'm afraid that we (and our worship) are like those dry bones more often than we'd like to admit. We, too, have sustained wounds, sometimes mortal wounds, in our souls and bodies. At least metaphorically, we may have been left for dead by those who did us in.

And we, too... Well, I'll speak for myself. *I* sometimes bring devastation into my own life. And I suspect that you do, too. We show up dry and parched, hopeless as a pile of bones, and wait for something to bring us to life.

Can *these* bones live? Can the liturgies that we offer to heal and comfort God's people resuscitate lifeless souls? We structure worship and bring all the "right" elements to it. Our congregations include florists and decorators who can bring the space to life with flowers and ribbons and banners. We have musicians who can evoke emotion and help create sacred space with beauty and timbre. Our preachers find our story in the stories of scriptures and offer it to us in our own context of healing and hope. But we know (don't we?) what determines if our worship is satisfying to our souls.

The bones came together. There were sinews on them, and flesh had come upon them, and skin had covered them; but there was no breath in them. (Ezekiel 37:8)

Breathe!

Come from the four winds, O breath, and breathe upon these slain, that they may live. (Ezekiel 37:9)

Selah! Pause. Wait. Take it in. Ruach, the breath, the Spirit.

I had the privilege to worship with an amazing newly formed congregation in Kenya. The congregation on the day I was there consisted of forty-eight women, fifty-three children, and eight men. The women are those who are excluded from worship in most other churches in the city: widows, single mothers, lesbians and prostitutes – all living in poverty. We gathered, as they do each

Sunday, in a dilapidated, tin-roofed community center. In what we might consider an unlikely place, all who were there on that day had a profound experience of the Spirit.

There was no stated order of worship. There was free singing and dancing and times of prayer, some vocalized, some silent. I preached. And in the silence, in the singing, in the dancing bodies of the children, was the animation of the Spirit. It was in my sermon, too – it blessed my preaching. And dry, tired, alienated people were refreshed and energized. Hope and brightness was restored, the beauty of God revealed.

Selah! Take it in. Ruach, the breath, the Spirit.

What might happen if our souls cried *Selah!* during our worship? And then we actually stopped and breathed in the silence, the stillness – savoring the flavor that we find?

What would happen if Selah became our practice during the week and we entered worship expectantly – knowing that we'll receive life when we stop, breathe, and savor the Spirit?

I wonder if we could also make Selah a verb; I will... *selah!* I will stop and invite the Spirit.

When we feel the word in our mouth or even consider it in our minds, may it call us to stillness and contemplation. Selah! Taste and see! Selah! Ruach. Breathe it in. Taste the stillness. Feel in your body the breath of the Spirit.

THE SUNDAYS AFTER PENTECOST

19

FAITHS AND FLAGS
Independence Day

Luke 10:1-11, 17-19

After this Jesus appointed seventy others and sent them on ahead of him in pairs to every town and place where he himself intended to go. He said to them, "The harvest is plentiful, but the laborers are few; therefore ask the Lord of the harvest to send out laborers into his harvest. Go on your way. See, I am sending you out like lambs into the midst of wolves. Carry no purse, no bag, no sandals; and greet no one on the road. Whatever house you enter, first say, 'Peace to this house!' And if anyone is there who shares in peace, your peace will rest on that person; but if not, it will return to you. Remain in the same house, eating and drinking whatever they provide, for the laborer deserves to be paid. Do not move about from house to house. Whenever you enter a town and its people welcome you, eat what is set before you; cure the sick who are there, and say to them, 'The kingdom of God has come near to you.' But whenever you enter a town and they do not welcome you, go out into its streets and say, 'Even the dust of your town that clings to our feet, we wipe off in protest against you. Yet know this: the kingdom of God has come near.'"

The seventy returned with joy, saying, "Lord, in your name even the demons submit to us!" He said to them, "I watched Satan fall from heaven like a flash of lightning. See, I have given you authority to tread on snakes and scorpions, and over all the power of the enemy."

༄

On this American Independence Day, patriotic anthems will be sung in congregations across this great land. Worshipers will hear messages about God and country that intermingle national mission and the mission of the gospel. In some places of worship, being American has been so interpolated into the biblical messages, America's stories so woven into the stories of ancient Israel, that it is difficult to distinguish them from one another. For many, the leap is short from the chosen people of Israel to the chosen people of America.

This Independence Day, we re-examine the relationship between our citizenship and our faith. We remember, for example, that "one nation under God" has not always been a part of the American Pledge of Allegiance to the Flag. In 1954, Congress added it in an attempt to link patriotism with religious piety, as Americans sought to be differentiated from the godless Communism of the Soviet Union.

And, as we know, Western Christianity is not the only religion to be wed to patriotism. Faiths and flags are intertwined around the globe, with some disastrous results. Viewing God, that energizing life and power of the universe, as the god of a nation has happened for centuries and around the world.

We know from the Hebrew scriptures that Yahweh was originally known only as the God of Israel. This led to wars in the name of Yahweh, killing and conquering not only in biblical times but throughout this Christian era. The Crusades were the Christian equivalent of Jihad, holy wars to the extreme that were meant to conquer the world for Christianity.

So, this is an uncomfortable juxtaposition: Independence Day and Sunday, our day of worship. What do we celebrate today?

What does it have to do with God? Just how do we as Christians participate in the public life of our nation without promoting a national or nationalistic religion?

We know that religious freedom is one of the hallmarks of our national identity. And we know that, over the last several decades, we have experienced the Christian Right's imposition of fundamentalist values and beliefs, which they would consider definitive of Christianity, or of being American.

This flies in the face of our religious liberty, presuming somehow that we are a single-religion nation. Everything else is suspect, unpatriotic, un-American.

In 2001, Captain James Yee was commissioned as one of the first Muslim chaplains in the US Army.

After September 11, he became a military spokesperson, educating soldiers about Islam. Subsequently Chaplain Yee served as the Muslim chaplain at Guantanamo Bay, where nearly seven hundred detainees were held.

In September 2003, after serving at Guantanamo for ten months with unrestricted access to the detainees and after receiving numerous awards for his service there, Chaplain Yee was secretly arrested on his way to meet his family for a routine leave. He was accused of espionage, of spying, and aiding the Taliban and Al Qaeda. He faced charges so severe that he was threatened with the death penalty. Yee spent seventy-six days in solitary confinement in a Navy prison and was treated in the same abusive way as the Guantanamo detainees.

In 2004, the United States government dropped all charges against him, stating that it had made a mistake in its original allegations. Then the government vindictively charged him with adultery and computer pornography. In the end, all criminal charges were dropped and Chaplain Yee's record wiped clean, but his reputation was tarnished, and what had been a promising military career was left in ruins. (Yee and Malloy)

How ironic that the U.S. constitution provides for freedom of religion! Based on its provisions, the United States should be a magnet for religious freedom, for pluralism. And yet, we ignore or punish deviations from what is considered the norm: a right-leaning form of Christianity.

But, you may ask, isn't America a Christian nation? The short answer is: no, not really. Several of those who laid our nation's foundations, including Thomas Jefferson and Benjamin Franklin, considered themselves Deists. Deism is based on nature and reason, not "revelation". Deism defers to no holy book, priests, rabbis, to reveal God's work and nature. Rather, God is realized by contemplating common sense and creation. A Deist's only prayers are prayers of thanksgiving and appreciation.

And yet, we maintain a clear identity as a single-faith nation that will not tolerate expressions of other faiths. A comparison of the regard for sacred texts tells the story. The Qur'an was abused and destroyed at Guantanamo Bay while the Christian Bible has been used to swear in jurors and witnesses in our judicial systems.

Is it possible to participate in our national life and our religious life without conflict? The New Testament is clear. If we speak of balancing our faith with our patriotism, creating co-primary loyalties, we simply do not hear the message of Christianity. The first Christian creedal statement "Jesus is Lord" was in direct defiance of the authoritarian role of the nation. Under Roman rule everyone, regardless of religion, was bound, under penalty of death, to declare, "Caesar is Lord." Christians could not pledge that kind of allegiance to Caesar without rejecting their under-standing of the place of Jesus in their lives. Many were executed for their failure to do so.

We must not, however, withdraw to our sanctuaries and leave participation in our civic life and governance to others. We must not choose one as the holy realm and relegate the other to a place of unholy unimportance. Rather, we must be clear about the good that we can do in this world and clear about the values and priorities to which our faith calls us. Then we exercise those values and priorities in service of the common good without imposing our religion and without shrinking from God's call to justice, healing, and inclusion. Our primary allegiance is to God; our values are the values that shaped Jesus' life.

Charles J. Chaput, archbishop of Denver, wrote in *The New York Times*:

> The Constitution does not, nor was it ever intended to, prohibit people or communities of faith from playing an active role in public life. Exiling religion from civic debate separates government from morality and citizens from their consciences. That road leads to politics without character, now a national epidemic.

We remember that Jesus sends a crowd of seventy disciples off, two by two, on a mission: to proclaim the kingdom of God and to heal. Clearly, the kingdom of God is a political term. The substance of the kingdom of God is freedom from domination. This is a freedom created by love, compassion, power, and justice: freedom not only for our souls, but for social and political realities as well.

Jesus tells the seventy not to take money, possessions, or food for the journey, perhaps to emphasize the mutuality of this different sort of kingdom, that all are capable of giving and receiving. Unlike representatives of other "kingdoms", they are to take no weapons, no flags, no national symbols, no recruiting officers. No symbols of domination or coercion or warfare announce this kingdom. The kingdom is beyond boundary of nation. It is God for the world and for the good of the world. You see, "seventy" probably represents the total number of nations in the world, all the nations. This is a message of inclusion, of non-violence in the face of antagonism, of blessing and peace for all.

When the seventy returned from their mission, they were ecstatic. They brought astounding reports of healing, peace, and liberation.

"Yes," replied Jesus, "while you were doing the work of peace and blessing, I saw Satan fall like lightning." In other words, the disciples knew they were spreading compassion and kindness, following Jesus' instructions by touching those in need, speaking peace and announcing God's care. While they knew they had experienced the power of God, they had no idea that their actions had cosmic implications. But Jesus told them their deeds of mercy and grace were bringing down all that is contrary to peace, all that is contrary to health and wholeness. They had the power to put the world right, to dispel the very powers that keep human beings from God's desire for humankind.

From our vantage point as followers of Jesus, can we offer ourselves and our action to put our nation and the world right? Our faith calls us to extend ourselves beyond the privacy of our churches to proclaim and work for the healing of our nation and the world, to bring the values and actions of healing and help to the sphere of public life by doing what we can to promote the gospel values of peace, inclusion, hope, and justice.

Churches and synagogues can take the lead; we can work toward closing the gap between belief and practice. We have the opportunity to turn professed faith into a lived-out faith which reflects the life and values of our spirituality.

What is it that we can do? We are frustrated – even angered – by the equation of public expressions of Christianity with fundamentalism. As progressive people of faith, we certainly don't want to do what fundamentalism has done. But we can pray, speak, and act.

We can pray, not for the supremacy of our nation, not for God's exclusive favor, but for peace and freedom, in thanksgiving and in petition for all the world. We can pray for our own courage and for clarity and boldness for those in places of influence.

Theologian Karl Barth said that "to clasp the hands in prayer is the beginning of an uprising against the disorder of the world." (Barth, 68)

We can speak. And act. Those on the religious left have nearly abandoned the voice of Christianity to those on the far right, and the religious right has come to be inseparable from unquestioning nationalistic loyalty. Questioning or disagreeing is often understood as un-American and unpatriotic. But we must question and challenge when we need to. If we could overcome our timidity and speak out with the authority that Jesus gave those who went out two by two, our actions would bring healing to our nation and new understanding of what it means to follow Jesus.

Could we move out into our world and into our civic life, doing what might seem small, in service of the common good and freedom for all? We could speak out, not only in gratitude for the privileges that we realize, but about the civil rights of all people. We could speak for those who do not breathe the air of freedom: those who are hungry and homeless, those who are living without healthcare, those who are trapped in the welfare cycle. We could bring hope to many with our advocacy. And we could change social realities in our communities.

What if we reminded our nation of its ethnic composition, recalling the free immigration that brought our ancestors to American soil? What if we said once again, "Give me your tired, your poor, your huddled masses, yearning to breathe free." (Lazarus, 58)

What if we connected our faith with affirmative action and reproductive rights, insisting, in the name of all that is just and holy, on the autonomy of women and people of color? What if we demanded the rights of workers to make a livable wage by not purchasing from companies that engage in unethical practices?

What if we heard Jesus' pronouncement on our action in our country: You have the power to put the world right, to dispel the very powers that keep human beings from all that God desires for us?

Lest we think we have no power, an example. This is Russia in August of 1991. A political coup threatened to engulf the country in a bloody civil war. Boris Yeltzin and a small group of defenders occupied the Russian White House and managed to face off an army of tanks and troops ready to attack. They miraculously put down the rebellion. The key element in this resistance was played by the *babushkas,* the "old women in the church", and their courageous public witness for peace.

These bandana-wearing old women, who had kept the Orthodox Christian church alive for years during the Soviet period, had been ridiculed over the years. Nothing could have seemed more pathetic; they were regarded as evidence of the eventual death of religion in the Soviet Union.

And yet on that critical night of August 20, 1991, when martial law was proclaimed and people were told to go to their homes, many of these women disobeyed and went immediately to the place of confrontation.

Some of them fed the resisters in a public display of support; others staffed medical stations. Some prayed for a miracle, while still others, astoundingly, climbed up onto tanks, peered through the slits at the men inside and told them there were new orders, these from God: *Thou shalt not kill.*

The men stopped the tanks. The attack never materialized, and by the third day, the tide had turned. (Billington, 120-122)

I bet Jesus saw Satan falling again. These women of the church embodied the principles and had the courage to exert the power that they had, and the faith to believe that they could work for the good of all. This is religion brought to political life without dogma or coercion.

I feel grateful on this Independence Day that I have had the privileges of living in a country that has afforded me a liberal education, voice and vote in governance, and freedom of thought and opinion, that has a high regard for civil liberties and for participation in public life, with separation of religion and state, and protection of religious liberty. Simultaneously, I am troubled that we sometimes view all this as God's exclusive blessing on our nation, that the lines of separation between religion and state are increasingly blurred by those who promote a new theocracy, that we don't always use the explicit freedom to critique and improve our country, and that we on the left keep our faith separate from our politics for fear of repeating the sins of the religious right. If Jesus were to send us out today, would we venture into the public sphere to offer hope and healing, to proclaim peace and justice?

As we celebrate religious freedom today, may we use that freedom to bring God's values to our nation. May God grant us the wisdom, discernment, clarity, and courage to fulfill this high calling to justice and peace.

20

THE GOD OF SMALL THINGS

Wisdom of Solomon 14:1-10

A person who is preparing to sail and about to voyage over raging waves calls upon a piece of wood more fragile than the ship that carries the sailor. For it was desire for gain that planned that vessel, and wisdom was the artisan who built it; but it is your providence, O God, that steers its course, because you have given it a path in the sea, and a safe way through the waves, showing that you can save from every danger, so that even a person who lacks skill may put to sea.

It is your will that works of your wisdom should not be without effect; therefore people trust their lives even to the smallest piece of wood, and passing through the billows on a raft they come safely to land. For even in the beginning, when arrogant giants were perishing, the hope of the world took refuge on a raft, and guided by your hand left to the world the seed of a new generation.

Selected verses from Matthew 10 and 13

Are not two sparrows sold for a penny? Yet not one of them will fall to the ground apart from God. And even the hairs of your head are all counted. So do not be afraid; you are of more value than sparrows.

Jesus put before them a parable: "The realm of heaven is like a mustard seed that some-one took and sowed in his field; it is the smallest of all the seeds, but when it has grown, it is the greatest of shrubs and becomes a tree, so that the birds of the air come and make nests in its branches." He told them another parable: "The realm of heaven is like yeast that a woman took and mixed in with three measures of flour until all of it was leavened...

"The realm of heaven is like treasure hidden in a field, which someone found and hid; then in his joy he goes and sells all that he has and buys that field.

"Again, the realm of heaven is like a merchant in search of fine pearls; on finding one pearl of great value, he went and sold all that he had and bought it."

❧

I THINK ABOUT small things when I get frustrated with myself for not accomplishing what I hope I will.

Here's how my thinking goes: Those I admire – friends who develop and use their gifts, who take time for kindness, who express their passions, create beauty with words or sound, tell stories with insight (and then run a marathon and write a book) – those people have precisely the same number of minutes in every day that I have. And it's in those minutes – even seconds – that the words and actions, the music and compassion come to life, take human shape. Holiness and hope are lived by human beings in those tiny moments, with a series of actions that can be done in hours and days.

Small things. Small moments. Brush strokes. Words. Thoughts. Rhythms.

The passage from the Wisdom of Solomon reminds us that we entrust our lives to the smallest piece of wood – a raft. And Jesus asks:

Are not two sparrows sold for a penny? Yet not one of them will fall to the ground apart from God. And even the hairs of your head are all counted. (Matthew 10:29-30)

The realm of heaven is like a mustard seed that someone took and sowed in his field; it is the smallest of all the seeds. (Matthew 13:31-32)

The obvious analogies and points are, of course, that it's not the tiny piece of wood in which we put our trust; that God who cares for the smallest sparrow surely cares for us; and that, like the acorn, great things can grow from small beginnings.

But there's more! Actual worth and meaning is often located in the small, not just the promise that it will grow into something large and spectacular.

The scriptures speak of the greater-than-relative value of other small, seemingly insignificant things: the widow's mite, the youngest son who's chosen to be king, David's dominance over Goliath, a cup of water given, God's still, small voice.

What are we to make of these clear choices to reference little things in this way that reorders what we somehow expect? After all, size matters in so much that we do. Bigger is better. We super-size, king- and queen-size. Left to our own devices, we might still see big cars as symbols of power and wealth.

Big churches, even, are viewed as monuments to successful leadership and maybe even divine favor.

And God for us is often the omnipotent one, hovering from heaven, interested in nations and galaxies. This image of God is about power, immensity, and might. We often think of God as revealed in grandeur, in drama, in the vastness of oceans and galaxies, and we assume that God calls a few really good people to know God and do profound world-transforming spiritual work of relieving hunger and accomplishing peace.

But I wonder if we miss something essential about the Love that sustains the universe when we make these assumptions.

Williams Jennings Bryan, the early twentieth-century politician turned religious fundamentalist, was best-known for his role as a prosecutor in the trial of Tennessee school teacher John Thomas Scopes. You'll remember that Scopes had taught the theory of evolution to his students in defiance of a state law prohibiting it. The defense attorney was Clarence Darrow. Bryan won the case, but died just a few weeks later. Darrow's tough cross-examination humiliated Bryan and dealt a hard blow to fundamentalism.

In the play *Inherit the Wind*, based on the Scopes trial, a news reporter, when hearing of Bryan's death, says to Clarence Darrow, "Why should we weep for him? He was a Bible-beating blowhard."

Darrow replies with compassion and says of Bryan, "A giant once lived in that body. But he got lost – lost because he was looking for God too high up and too far away." (Lawrence and Lee, 128)

In creation, provision, and choice, God has regard for what is small, ordinary, overlooked, seemingly insignificant. God is with us in the moment-by-momentness of our lives, in bits of time and substance, in small needs and in ordinary events. God is there and speaking. If we lose sight of this, we, like William Jennings Bryan, risk unwittingly distorting the One who offers profound love and beauty, meaning and life in the tiny and mundane.

Now, I'm not talking about limiting God or even ourselves. Neither am I suggesting that we keep ourselves small when bigness is what's needed. Rather, I'm calling us to be aware of and appreciate the images that elevate the daily and mundane to the status of holy revelation. God is revealed, known, and experienced in small things.

I venture to say that most of us don't make bread. Maybe some have never even witnessed the transforming power of yeast. Just a pinch is all that's needed. We don't use masses of anything to make bread rise, to give it texture and softness. Rather, a little does the magic. More spoils it.

When we get right down to it, we know the power of small things. We know that two seconds' worth of comments from our parents – either supportive or critical – can shape our lives: "Jeffrey can't sing." "You know Robert has the looks – but Jill, well… she's the smart one." "You always do that." Or maybe we heard, "I'm so proud of you!" Or, "You do the kindest things." "I couldn't ask for a more wonderful son."

When I think of small things that have made a difference in my life, two incidents come to mind:

The first happened when I was teaching music in a Catholic girls' school in Minnesota. One of the sisters whom I deeply admired was in the hospital. I went to visit, with great nervousness and a small African violet. I found the room, knocked, and timidly entered. Sister Mary Frances and I talked for an hour. It was one of those conversations that you wish would never end but seems to last only ten minutes. The following week, I received a one-sentence note from Sister Mary Frances that rocked my world. It simply said, "What a delight to meet Jesus again in you." This was a small blessing that expanded my theology and still brings life to me.

The second incident happened around the same time. My two children were small and our family was preparing for a two-thousand-mile, cross-country move. I was finishing up my teaching year, saying goodbye to friends and work that I didn't want to leave, and packing to move. I felt overwhelmed and despondent. A number of friends generously said to call if I needed anything. But my friend Mary Ann just showed up at my door one day and said: "Give me your dirty laundry." Now it doesn't get much smaller or more mundane than that. But the friendship and empathy in that sentence taught me that small actions embody great love.

I'm sure you remember little actions or words that influenced your life. Perhaps others remember little things you've said or done – for good or for ill. What we do matters as well – a word, a look, can be life-giving or devastating. We may not think that little things we do or say impact others, but they do.

Like when our insensitive evil twin comes around and we give her control of our gossipy tongues. Or we somehow think there's not enough drama in the world, so we spread a little – stretch the truth just a bit, enough to get a response. Small actions with enough power to break a heart, sever a friendship, or distract a church from its important work in the world.

Imagine now if we resolved today to turn this around, if we did a little something each day to offer grace or kindness to another: a word, a gift. Encouragement, praise, even a touch – small things that can be done in a moment and cost us nothing. If we did, others would be lifted and we would be changed.

You've probably read those words of Mother Teresa:

Don't look for big things; just do small things with great love. The smaller the thing, the greater must be our love. (Teresa, 34)

And Jesus said that "the realm of heaven is like a mustard seed." (Matthew 13:31) It will grow like a weed! (Actually, it is a weed. That's part of the charm of the story that Jesus tells, and something to ponder.)

Then we all, I assume, have those times when *we* feel small, when we think – even momentarily – that we don't matter, that any good we might manage to do is so small that it's totally insignificant. Our perspective is distorted and our lives seem trivial and we decide that we don't really mean much to anyone. Or is it just me?

In these times, I need the God of small things. I need to hold fast to the One who assures us that we do matter: our worries, our disturbing thoughts, our secret dreams, our insecurities. They matter. They're life, after all, life that's lived in moments, hours, and days. Small, important lives are how love is known and healing is accomplished.

Indian author Arundhati Roy wrote a book with the same title that I've given this sermon, *The God of Small Things*. Although this is a culturally complex saga with embedded themes of home, migration, social caste barriers, and national identity, Roy tells the tale with the meaning in the details.

It's the story of seven-year-old Estha and his twin sister, Rahel, who live in a small Indian village. The tale is an interplay between their childhood and adulthood, but it focuses on the little things in their childhoods – both as they happen and as they're remembered during their adulthood. Their mother, Ammu, struggling with a cross-caste relationship, neglects them and says cruel things to them. So, they decide to leave home until their mother remembers how much she loves them.

They find sanctuary in an abandoned house across the lake from their village. Their most valuable possessions offer comfort and grounding: a plastic goose, a stuffed bear with loose button eyes, two ballpoint pens (souvenirs from London) and a toy watch.

Do you hear it? The meaning – the comfort, identity, and memory – resides in small things. The smallest things somehow embody the most important.

Poet Deena Metzger wrote so beautifully:

Each day is a tapestry, threads of broccoli, promotion, couches, children, politics, shopping, building, planting, thinking interweave in intimate connection with insistent cycles of birth, existence, and death. We can become so focused on our own accomplishments that we will not even see the holy, sacred, healing grace of God present all around us. (Metzger, 7)

May we find this God of and in small, momentary, ordinary things: a truth told, a hand touched, a moment of calm, an unexplained hope. The wonder and meaning and beauty are all around and within. They are in the intricate details of each day. May God give us eyes to see, imaginations to ponder, and courage to participate in the small things of God.

21

SAVED

Matthew 14:22-31 from *The Message*, an adaptation by Eugene Peterson

As soon as the meal was finished, Jesus told the disciples to get in the boat and go on ahead to the other side while he dismissed the people. With the crowd dispersed, he climbed the mountain so he could be by himself and pray. He stayed there alone, late into the night.

Meanwhile, the boat was far out to sea when the wind came up against them and they were battered by the waves. At about four o'clock in the morning, Jesus came toward them walking on the water. They were scared out of their wits. "A ghost!" they said, crying out in terror.

But Jesus was quick to comfort them. "Courage, it's me. Don't be afraid." Peter, suddenly bold, said, "Teacher, if it's really you, call me to come to you on the water." He said, "Come ahead."

Stepping out of the boat, Peter walked on the water to Jesus. But when he looked down at the waves churning beneath his feet, he lost his nerve and started to sink. He cried, "Save me!"

Jesus didn't hesitate. He reached down and grabbed his hand.

ℰↄ

You know the story. The sea is stormy; the disciples are afraid. Jesus walks out on the sea; the disciples think it's a ghost. But Jesus assures them: "Take heart, it is I; have no fear." Then audacious Peter shouts: "If it's really you, bid me come to you on the water."

Well, Peter steps out. Walks on the water. For a minute.

Suddenly Peter is sinking, caught up in the stormy sea. "Save me," he calls out to Jesus. Jesus lifts him up, saves him from sinking and drowning.

This is the story. We know it. And we can tell that this isn't just about Peter. It's our story, too. It's a portrait of the human predicament. We step out into the choppy waters of trouble, of impossible relationships, of spiritual turmoil, of pain, suffering, doubt, selfishness, arrogance, self-deception, brokenness, despair, and failure. It's the story of human beings who, like Peter, need to be *saved* from drowning in the swelling sea.

Peter is us, showing us that we can do incredible things in the world – impossible things. And yet, we sometimes find ourselves sinking, struggling, drowning. We need to be saved.

Now, this is a concept that we liberals don't spend too much time contemplating. It's been the property of evangelicals and fundamentalists and we've pretty well kept our distance. It's the defining religious question for some, isn't it? "Are you saved?"

The answer, of course, is based on varying criteria, depending on one's tradition. If you're evangelical, the question might mean, "Have you been 'born again?'" But, if you're Catholic, it could mean, "Have you been baptized?"

A Disciples of Christ theologian has described salvation as:

Forgiveness for all manner of human gone-wrongness, wholeness and healing, peace of mind and peace in society, freedom from oppression and anxiety, eternal life in the world to come, enriched meaning and purpose in a more abundant life here and now. God's victory over everything that is death-dealing, enslaving, and alienating about human existence.

Put that way, I think I would like some!

Salvation is clearly a Biblical theme. The words for "save," "salvation" and "savior" occur six hundred and thirty-one times in the New Revised Standard Version of the Bible. Christianity is a salvific religion. It's about being changed – lifted from our despair to hope – about dying and living again. And our religious roots are in Judaism, also a salvific religion with poignant concepts of redemption, liberation, and healing.

The defining event of redemption and salvation in Judaism is the Exodus event, through which the people of Israel are delivered out of slavery, led out of hostile territory from the hands of an enemy and a life of captivity, and brought to freedom and safety. In fact, God is defined in this way: "I am Yahweh your God, who brought you out of the land of Egypt." (Exodus 20:2)

God is not only the world's Creator but the world's Savior. Christ is not only teacher and example, but one who saves. The people of God are not only a supportive and loving group, but are those saved by God's love and grace and called to do "saving" work in the world.

Questions abound! We don't only hear, "Are you saved?" We might also wonder what it means to be saved, why I might want to be saved, just how that comes about or if it's a direct result of a loving God. We might also want to consider just what it could be that we're saved from.

Salvation is an establishment or re-establishment of health, safety, or security. It is accomplished through acts of deliverance, healing, liberation, rescue, and transformation. We are saved from that which oppresses us, from hopelessness, from our own foibles, from guilt, despair, self-centeredness, shame, and arrogance. Salvation is the holy, merciful, mystical process by which our life is made new, offering us a place of beginning again.

In a book on salvation in early Christianity, Gail Paterson Corrington says that:

> Only the Divine – whether located in heaven or in some extraordinary way within a person, has the power necessary to overcome the hostile forces that produce feelings of helplessness and powerlessness.
>
> The experience of salvation, therefore, is an experience whereby the saved participate in the power of the Divine. One's existence is transformed from powerless to powerful. (Corrington, 46)

Historically, salvation is from the power of the Pharaoh, that which keeps us captive and over which we seem to have no control. In the ministry of Jesus, the experience of salvation moves from the redemption of Israel as a nation to the salvation – the healing and restoration of individuals. Remember how Jesus brought this salvific touch to the centurion, the Syrophoenician woman, to Zacchaeus and the nameless woman at the well. Each of these was in profound need; they received hope, dignity, challenge, healing, and redeemed lives from Jesus.

Why might I want to be saved? The overwhelming message of the church continues to be that we need to be saved so that we can get to heaven. But salvation is so much more. It's the healing work of God's grace showered on us through a variety of means, the possibility of living a meaningful life.

We have experienced salvation when, against all odds, we are relieved of habits that keep us from fully living, when we experience healing, hope, wholeness, and freedom from any source. We are saved when we know we're not in this alone, when we realize that God is with us.

Ralph Waldo Emerson, in his address called "Miracles", captures our curiosity with his contention that miracles are monstrous. He implies that the existence of miracles could only be a distraction to a healthy spiritual life. They would poke themselves up out of the level of the everyday world and selfishly grab all the limelight. Miracles would proclaim that only here, only right now, and only in this place is something divine happening.

Emerson argues that concentrating divinity in only a few special places makes us discount the divinity of the everyday.

Could we say the same of salvation? That salvation is all around us and in us, that it has many messengers and midwives, and that we need salvation in each day?

When I was a child, our family belonged to a church that observed the practice of "altar calls" at the close of each service. Those present were invited to come to the altar as a sign of a need, as a form of confession, or to witness a change or resolve that they were making – to accept God's salvation in some way. Many people walked that aisle only once or, maybe, twice in their lives, but there was one man at Central Baptist Church who came to the altar, red-faced and sobbing, about one Sunday a month.

Most people thought he was a bit unstable, but I wonder if he was onto something: that God's salvation, God's hope, healing, forgiveness, blessing, balm for our wounds, and remaking of our gone-wrong selves is something we need every time we begin to sink.

In twelve-step meetings, the slogan is often heard: "Just for today." This mantra emphasizes the currency of the gift of sobriety, the salvation that is new every morning. We need it to live abundant lives, to receive another chance, a new beginning. We human beings need to find healing, hope, and freedom from that which threatens to pull us under.

Want it?

Perhaps you know about those violent waves that bash your

ship, that sinking feeling when we need to be saved from the undertow of self-serving motives, of addiction, of negativity, of resentment, of despair. It's not a matter of passively waiting until something mysterious happens in your heart. We can simply announce our need, as Peter did: *Save me!*

Just as we are being saved daily, we can be partners with God in offering salvation as well. Deep waters of loneliness, exclusion, pain, sufferings small and large, threaten so many. The undertow of spiritual despair and apathy pulls those we love into the depths. We all have opportunities to step into threatening waters and bring healing, hope, and life – salvation – to another.

What might your salvation be today? From what do you need to be saved? What is pulling you under? Causing you to sink?

Salvation is all around us and within us. It's new every morning for each day's need.

May we receive it with gladness and pass it on with compassion and joy!

22

CULTURE OF COMPLAINT

Ephesians 4:25-32

So then, putting away falsehood, let all of us speak the truth to our neighbors, for we are members of one another. Be angry but do not sin; do not let the sun go down on your anger, and do not make room for the devil. Thieves must give up stealing; rather let them labor and work honestly with their own hands, so as to have something to share with the needy. Let no evil talk come out of your mouths, but only what is useful for building up, as there is need, so that your words may give grace to those who hear. And do not grieve the Holy Spirit of God, with which you were marked with a seal for the day of redemption. Put away from you all bitterness and wrath and anger and wrangling and slander, together with all malice, and be kind to one another, tender-hearted, forgiving one another, as God in Christ has forgiven you.

John 6:35, 41-44

Jesus said to them, "I am the bread of life. Whoever comes to me will never be hungry, and whoever believes in me will never be thirsty."

The Jews began to complain about him because he said, "I am the bread that came down from heaven." They were saying, "Is not this Jesus, the son of Joseph, whose father and mother we know? How can he now say, 'I have come down from heaven'?" Jesus answered them, "Do not complain among yourselves. No one can come to me unless drawn by the One who sent me; and I will raise that person up on the last day."

❧

TODAY, WE TURN to Paul's letter to the Ephesian congregation to explore the nature of life in community and the opportunities to exercise kindness and love that living in community offers us.

Now, I don't think I'm being overly optimistic when I express the conviction that most of us want to be kind. We want to do the right thing. Most of the time, most of us have reasonably pure hearts and decent motives.

But what comes out of our mouths is often quite another thing. Our speech and behaviors don't always match our inner intentions to be fine, upstanding, honorable people. Of course, none of us give in to complaining, grumbling and blaming all the time. But most of us do some of the time. We moan and complain and take little pieces of information about each other and use it to boost our own egos. We pick at each other and at life. We do – at the most insignificant things. We complain when things aren't what we like or when others don't do things our way. We scrutinize their motives and imagine the worst – all the while acting as if we are beyond reproach. Most of us fall into these behaviors from time to time. It's human nature. And we've all heard or been the subject of others' petty – sometimes destructive – complaints.

Even Jesus was on the receiving end of such harshness. This incident from John's gospel wasn't the only time he was the target of complaints and belittling accusations. But, in this story, Jesus extends himself to his accusers; he offers himself openly and boldly – says he'll be there for them, connect with them. He tells them that he's come from God to be the bread of life for them – to nourish and renew.

And they complained about his offer! They picked it apart, assuming that he was being literal about coming from heaven.

They didn't take the time to reflect on what he really meant. Rather, they basically said, "Who does he think he is to say he came from heaven? We know who his parents are!"

Even Jesus isn't immune to the over-dissecting criticism of the naysayers, those who have let themselves slip into a destructive culture of criticism that blinds them to the gift of God that is right before their eyes.

This was probably no surprise to Jesus. He had read the Bible – the stories of the prophets and Moses and the people who complained against Moses, even in the face of his honest and faithful leadership.

Those who had been liberated from slavery grumbled as Moses led them toward the Promised Land. Remember their woe-is-me cries? "We were better off as slaves in Egypt than starving in the desert!"

Now, just a clarification here about complaining and saying what's on our minds: many of us have been on the other side of this complaint fence. That is, we weren't "allowed" to speak our resistance, to name our troubles. We have been shushed, shamed, or scolded into silence. But we've learned – some of us – that we need to speak out even when it goes against the grain. And that's a good thing.

It's a good thing unless grumbling takes us over and becomes a way of life that infects our spirits and keeps us in a constant state of blaming and perceiving negativity. It's a positive attribute unless the shadows of complaint block the sun of blessing that's shining on us, unless our moaning becomes a shield that we use to protect ourselves from facing our own fallibility and error. And, while it's important for us to express our feelings, we need to keep perspective, realizing that our feelings are *our* truth – but rarely are they the whole truth. The shield of complaining and blaming can keep us in a place of self-righteousness. The shield is around us while the arrows fly at others.

There is that assumption in complaint, you know. The assumption is this: I can criticize because I know better. I could do it better, make better judgments, have purer motives, probably look better doing it, and behave in the unquestionably right and righteous way.

The problem is – of course – that this is simply not the whole truth about ourselves or others. Well, that's one problem with living in an internal culture of complaint.

Another problem is (like those Moses-following grumblers in Exodus; like those to whom Paul was writing at the church in Ephesus; and like those who picked at the words of Jesus) that wrangling, judging, accusing, grumbling, gossiping, and moaning keep us from seeing and realizing the praiseworthy beauty and abundance that are right in front of us and within us.

Paul is honest with the church folks in Ephesus. He knows that if they care deeply and believe passionately, there will be conflict. Disagreements, different ways, and bold actions will occasionally provoke anger. We can't gather a bunch of passionately devoted people and not eventually clash in some way. Paul isn't naïve. But he urges them to temper their response, to let anything they say be honest, useful, kind, and full of grace.

And he ties these tall demands to their realization that God offers constant grace to them. They – and we – have all had love extended to us and grace and forgiveness, many times over, I suspect. And not only from God – but from others as well. Is it too much to ask that we pass it on?

But not in a "can't we all just be nice" way! And not without truth – even when it's tough. That's how Paul began this section of his letter, encouraging the Ephesian congregation to speak the truth to each other.

We aren't naïve either. We know, if we've been in any church (or group, for that matter) for long, that we do get irritated. And sometimes we get irritated with the same person for the umpteenth time about the very same behavior. And so, every time "her" name comes up, it makes my blood boil and I just have to let it out. If "he" interrupts one more time, I can feel the desire to call him names rising!

We all have feelings – sometimes strong feelings – when we try to live in community with each other. Our buttons get pushed. We feel left out or singled out. And so we whine and moan to anyone who will listen. But sometimes it takes us over and we can't see anything good about "those" people.

Now, I'm not going to simply say to you, "Stop complaining. Quit feeling sorry for yourself. Never make judgments about each other ever again. Stop it." I'm not going to tell you to stuff your feelings or insist that you just be nice and pretend that things are okay with you if they aren't. Nope, I'm not going to say that.

I'm not even going to suggest that criticism is a bad thing. On the contrary, we need a moral compass that differentiates among behaviors – ours and others'.

Rather, I'd like to suggest two spiritual remedies to the myopic culture of complaint, this infection of non-reflectively seeing the glass half empty, the unexamined imperative to see the negative first – often to the exclusion of the positive – and the horrible symptoms of bitterness, resentment, anger, alienation from others, and an argumentative, critical spirit.

The first remedy is gratitude, a specific sort of gratitude: the deep and constant realization that we have been given the benefit of the doubt and a measure of grace that restores our souls and our dignity – even when we don't "deserve" it.

Standing just behind gratitude is humility – that is, recognizing our own humanity and fallibility. When we're clear about our own humanity – both our gifts and our failures – and remember the grace we've been offered, we become ready to offer that kindness and acceptance to others – even if they don't "deserve" it!

Gratitude overflows from all that we've received and empowers us to offer grace to others. Where gratitude abounds, grace emerges, and complaining fades.

The second remedy for a self-and-other destructive culture of complaint is compassion. I am convinced that the opposite of complaining is not simply to remain silent, to stuff our feelings, or to pretend that we don't react to others' words and actions. Rather, I think the opposite of complaining is compassion. Compassion is aware of and sensitive to the underlying feelings and sufferings of the other. Compassion assumes that the one who irritates you needs your love and kindness much more than your criticism. And it assumes that you have the power to heal some deep wound in another person by offering grace instead of grumbling.

Poet Miller Williams writes:

Have compassion for everyone you meet. What seems conceit, bad manners, or cynicism is always a sign of things no ears have heard, no eyes have seen. You do not know what wars are going on down there where the spirit meets the bone. (Williams, 55)

Take a moment to remember when someone has given you the benefit of the doubt, offered you grace and forgiveness when you've done something less than stellar. Then consider what you could do that would make someone who has offended you in some way equally grateful to you.

I've found help in one of the principles in Stephen Covey's book, *The Seven Habits of Highly Effective People*. Habit 5 is this: "Seek first to understand, then to be understood." (Covey, 235) This is an expression of compassion, a way of offering the grace of God to another, an opportunity for love in action.

Paul begins this passage in his letter to the Ephesians with an admonition to speak the truth in love. If we do this, if we say what seems to be truth and we do so with the primary value of love, we reduce our need to grumble, because we've actually done something to remedy the problem. Tell the truth as you see it. Say it. Say it to the person to whom it needs to be said (rather than to twelve others).

Failing to speak the truth in a loving and appropriate way to the appropriate person is one of the deep roots of the culture of complaint. It might go something like this:

I offend you, and you tell Sue, who is irate and tells Mark, who gets in a huff and remembers when I offended him three years ago. Meanwhile, Mark thinks Sue is out of line for telling something that didn't happen to her. He calls Karen to express his outrage – and takes the opportunity to call Sue a few choice names. All this time, I (the original offender) am clueless. You're all angry and I'm not sure why you're grumbling about each other.

The culture of complaint keeps us from seeing each other's goodness and it keeps us from honestly facing our own capability to be just as irritating and prone to mistakes as everyone else. So, we say whatever it takes to make ourselves feel better. That may be blaming someone for excluding us, rather than taking the responsibility and privilege of initiating and reaching out to others. It may be taking a grain of truth and using it to make someone else look bad so that we can feel alright about ourselves. Or it may be gossiping to let others know that we have inside information.

How do we speak to and about each other?

Our answer to this question is an indicator of our individual spiritual maturity and, like a thermometer, it measures our health and may signal an infection in the body.

One of Paul's most compelling images of the church is the

image of One Body. In a stunning reference to Jesus' words at the Last Supper, Paul tells us that we are the body of Christ. Each of us is an indispensable part and all the parts work together to be the real presence of Christ to each other and in the world: the healing, hope-offering, uplifting, honest, compelling presence of Christ.

The infection of complaint and judgment and thoughtless speech makes the body of Christ sick. It diminishes our power to live in love. And it shrouds our eyes, preventing us from seeing each other's humanity and needs, gifts and goodness. And it ultimately dims our vision of the light of God.

When I first moved to Oregon a number of years ago, I had difficulty adjusting to the cloudiness and rain. I complained about it. A lot. Eventually, I would just wake up to yet another overcast day and feel grumbly and cranky. It became an attitude of my life. *Until.* Until a sun-break would come!

If you've lived in the Pacific Northwest, you know about sun-breaks – those glorious moments when the sun erupts through the clouds with brilliance and palpable warmth. They took my breath away. In fact, I didn't realize that grumbling and negativity owned me, dominated my mood, until the sun broke through and shed light on it all. In that sudden light, I could see clearly. I know it sounds like overstatement, but it's true that hope and optimism flooded my soul.

So it is when we have been dulled and jaded by complaining and grumbling and criticizing. The clouds and shadows shroud us in such negativity that we can't see clearly. We don't even know that we've been living without gratitude and compassion.

But gratitude and compassion are our remedies. When we take them up first – rather than jumping to complaining conclusions – we may just find that the blessing is ours. We'll be showered with grace and offered the opportunity to pass it on.

We'll be offered the bread of life – the self-giving, other-loving Jesus way – to feed our own souls. And we'll find gratitude and compassion enough to offer light to another.

The Dalai Lama encourages us with this simple statement: "Be kind whenever possible. It is always possible." And it's medicine for our souls and our community.

23

BREAD IS RISING

1 Kings 19:1-8

Ahab told Jezebel all that Elijah had done, and how he had killed all the prophets with the sword. Then Jezebel sent a messenger to Elijah, saying, "So may the gods do to me, and more also, if I do not make your life like the life of one of them by this time tomorrow." Then he was afraid; he got up and fled for his life, and came to Beer-sheba, which belongs to Judah; he left his servant there. But he himself went a day's journey into the wilderness, and came and sat down under a solitary broom tree. He asked that he might die: "It is enough; now, O Lord, take away my life, for I am no better than my ancestors." Then he lay down under the broom tree and fell asleep.

Suddenly an angel touched him and said to him, "Get up and eat." He looked, and there at his head was a cake baked on hot stones, and a jar of water. He ate and drank, and lay down again. The angel of the Lord came a second time, touched him, and said, "Get up and eat, otherwise the journey will be too much for you." He got up, and ate and drank; then he went in the strength of that food forty days and forty nights to Horeb the mount of God.

John 6:35, 48-51

Jesus said to them, "I am the bread of life. Whoever comes to me will never be hungry, and whoever believes in me will never be thirsty.

"I am the bread of life. Your ancestors ate the manna in the wilderness, and they died. This is the bread that comes down from heaven, so that one may eat of it and not die. I am the living bread that came down from heaven. Whoever eats of this bread will live forever; and the bread that I will give for the life of the world is my flesh."

൚

THE BIBLE IS chock-full of bread stories: the saga of Moses and the manna in the wilderness; the Passover story of the unrisen bread that the people of Israel took with them; the bread of angels that fed the prophet Elijah; Jesus' feeding of the five thousand with five loaves and two fish. The word of God is compared to bread that sustains our spirits, Jesus refers to himself as the Bread of Life, and the Syrophoenician woman demands the children's metaphorical breadcrumbs from under the table.

Bread: Substance of life.

Basic to every culture with its connection to the earth.

Through the miracle of yeast, multiplying and spreading through the whole loaf, the bread rises, producing warmth, change, nourishment.

The image of bread brings together a physical experience and a spiritual reality.

Earthy bread.

Spiritual food.

Bread of heaven.

Bread of life.

Our story from Kings tells of the prophet Elijah running for his life – even though he's just led a campaign to overturn idolatrous religion! In her defeat, Jezebel, the queen of Israel, is intent on killing Elijah for destroying the cult that she had established among the Jews. Elijah flees to the wilderness where, overcome with depression, he prays to God to end his life.

In Elijah's mind, he had failed; his life was not worth living. He had done what he thought he could do to offer Yahweh's life-giving covenant. And all it got him was a death sentence. Today, we might say that Elijah was suffering from severe depression.

In the wilderness, Elijah lay down under the broom tree and fell asleep. But a messenger – some translations say "an angel" – touched him and told him to get up and eat. He found at his head a cake baked on hot stones, and a jar of water. He ate and drank, and lay down again. Still, he couldn't face his life, couldn't yet move.

The messenger came a second time, touched him, and said, "Get up and eat, otherwise the journey will be too much for you." Once again, Elijah got up, and ate and drank. Strengthened, he traveled to the mountain of God.

Elijah was exhausted – spiritually, physically, emotionally. He was distraught and despairing, spiritually ill, in need of healing and rest, nurture and nourishment.

Bread.

Spiritual food.

Source of energy and strength.

We can't make it without this bread. The journey will be too much for us.

Holy food.

Presence of God.

Mystery and mercy that relieves fear and breathes hope when we lose the will and the way.

When does *bread* – when does *food* – become that which revives our very lives? When does it become bread of angels and bread of life? The quick, churchy answer is "at this communion table".

But I remember Christmas day at my gran and granddad's house. We began with Christmas breakfast, but lunch had been long underway! Lunch included turkey and ham and vegetables from the past summer's harvest. There was stuffing, and pies and cakes filled the top of the sideboard. Lunch seemed to segue right into dinner as leftovers from lunch became yet another feast.

The day was fueled by the laughter of cousins, the caring

touches of aunts and uncles, the loving preparation of favorite dishes by grandmothers and mothers, music from my uncle's guitar, and jokes and stories. The nurturing of that table has lasted a lifetime: the warmth and love, the wisdom shared still forms a generation of our family.

This is bread of angels. Bread of life.

When I was a school teacher, I had a student called Rachel. Rachel's wealthy, work-obsessed parents had purchased an apartment near her high school and moved her in there to live on her own – away from the family – when she was only fifteen. Of course, she felt neglected, alone. Rachel's response, her outcry, was to act out with a radical, punk appearance simply for shock value. Her pink spiky hair shouted, *Notice me! Pay attention!*

Rachel got involved with the theatre group at the school, where she was but one of many expressive, artistic students. There she was embraced, seen for her quirky, witty self, and valued. To say that Rachel was "born again" just by being known isn't an exaggeration. She was nourished with attention, with affection.

This, too, is bread of salvation. Bread of life!

Have you been there? Sad. Hopeless. Despairing. Exhausted?

Then you know that a word of companionship in the silence of loneliness is indeed the *bread of angels!* Or perhaps you've received assurance of forgiveness in the wilderness of alienation and hurt. This is *the very bread of life!* Or maybe you've felt a gesture of kindness that breaks through grief: *bread of salvation!*

Jesus said to them:

"I am the bread of life. Your ancestors ate the manna in the wilderness, and they died.

"This is the bread that comes down from heaven, so that one may eat of it and not die.

"I am the living bread that came down from heaven."

I met Barbara when I was working in a women's prison. She was incarcerated for committing vehicular homicide. She fell asleep at the wheel, crossed the median, and hit another car head-on. Barbara had lived a decent life but had an Elijah experience in prison. "I'm worthless – nothing left. Just let me die and get it over with!" She was at the bottom, seeing no point in her life – or in life in general.

Barbara came along to the choir that I directed, just to occupy her time. The choir often traveled to churches to sing concerts during worship services. Their presence among the people in congregations raised awareness about incarcerated women and gave many of the women an outlet for self-expression, a way to tell their stories and claim their faith.

One night during a concert in a Pentecostal church, a larger-than-life, seventy-something man stood up in the congregation and prayed for the women. Compassion and concern flowed from each word as he spoke fervently. He prayed that God would give them hope somehow and new life. Barbara felt weak all over and held in the arms of God. In his prayer and in his voice and in his faith, she found the bread she needed to stay alive. The Spirit poured over her and she knew that God wanted her to live. She believed – for the first time in years – that her life could have purpose.

Bread of life! Substance of hope.

Bread – in the form of community, of family, of therapy or rest.

Bread that renews and restores us to sanity.

"Come to me, all you that are weary and carry heavy burdens, and I will give you rest." (Matthew 11:28)

Several years ago, I experienced a deep betrayal, a life-threatening action from someone I trusted. I was in absolute despair – unable to function, unable even to ask for the help I so desperately needed, unable to find anything to ease my pain, to solve my dilemma, unable, even, to pray. Until one choir rehearsal night, the music broke through.

> E'en so, Christ Jesus, quickly come
> And night shall be no more.
> They need no light, no lamp, nor sun
> For Christ will be their all! (Manz)

I fed on the melody, the harmony, the text. I had memorized this piece of music years before, but hadn't needed it until then. In the mystery of grace, I began to find a bit of comfort.

My Bread of Life. Hope of salvation!

"I am the bread of life," Jesus said. "Feed on me."

Feed on grace. Eat of the mystery and mercy.

Like the family gathered at the holiday table, the presence of God – the touch of love – can feed and hold us.

How long has it been since you've eaten spiritual bread? I'm not speaking of communion but manna of the heart, a feast of the Spirit.

My friend D'Anna recently told me that her pastor suggested that she spend five minutes each day with Jesus – not God, but Jesus. The idea was to commune with, to feed on, the presence of Jesus the healer, the one who sees you and looks deep within, who knows you and feeds you lavishly.

God's intention is that all are fed.

What table is spread before you? What sumptuous feast awaits you – ready to feed your hungry soul?

It's ready.

The table is prepared, and bread is rising even now.

24

WORDS

Mark 7:24-35

From there he set out and went away to the region of Tyre. He entered a house and did not want anyone to know he was there. Yet he could not escape notice, but a woman whose little daughter had an unclean spirit immediately heard about him, and she came and bowed down at his feet. Now the woman was a Gentile, of Syrophoenician origin. She begged him to cast the demon out of her daughter. He said to her, "Let the children be fed first, for it is not fair to take the children's food and throw it to the dogs." But she answered him, "Sir, even the dogs under the table eat the children's crumbs." Then he said to her, "For saying that, you may go – the demon has left your daughter." So she went home, found the child lying on the bed, and the demon gone.

Then he returned from the region of Tyre, and went by way of Sidon towards the Sea of Galilee, in the region of the Decapolis. They brought to him a deaf man who had an impediment in his speech; and they begged him to lay his hand on him. He took him aside in private, away from the crowd, and put his fingers into his ears, and he spat and touched his tongue. Then looking up to heaven, he sighed and said to him, "Ephphatha," that is, "Be opened." And immediately his ears were opened, his tongue was released, and he spoke plainly.

એલ

WORDS CAN CHANGE everything. Do you recall what someone said that sparked changes in you? Have you spoken words with life-changing or life-shattering power?

Our religious heritage calls us to consider the spoken word, the written word and the power of the Word. Jews refer to themselves as People of the Word, and Christians look to Jesus as The Word, the Logos of God.

Word is expression; that is, it manifests the essence of the speaker or writer. For many of us, the Word of God is found in the life-giving messages of the scriptures and beyond. Words are one deep way in which we know others and ourselves.

The important phrases "coming to voice" or "finding our voices" are used powerfully in feminist and liberation movements to speak of being in touch with our true selves and no longer being silenced by culture, custom, and oppression.

Now, I know people who cannot speak: some are deaf; others are unable to speak because of other maladies. But I have never known a person who did not have language, who is cut off from all interchange. However, I have known people who cannot hear, and have been at points in my own life when I could not hear the truth about myself, the truth about a situation or a relationship, when I was unable to listen to perspectives different from my own, could not even hear voices of love.

I have also suffered periods of time when I could not speak. I could not express my ideas for fear of rejection. Revelation of my own personal truths, even to myself, presented the possibility of loss so great that my tongue was frozen in my mouth.

Sometimes expressing the truth or the emotion, or the opinion or the dream that we hold inside is impossible for us. We are not silent by choice; we are emotionally or spiritually deaf and mute and we wish it were not so.

For many, speaking our truth – speaking at all – is a courageous act, especially for those who are marginalized in any way. For some who grew up in homes with heavy-handed parental authority, even to speak when one was not spoken to was a courageous act, an act of risk and daring. The causes of our frozen tongues, of our silence when we long to be able to speak, are varied and multi-dimensional: some of us feel constrained and silenced by those who refuse to listen. Many deal with some *ism*: racism, sexism, classism, or ableism that would suppress and silence our voices. Others hold a great censor within us, that inner sense that we must not speak. We struggle to reach a point of confidence, a point of self-affirmation that convinces us that we have the right to speak and that our voices are valid.

In this gospel story, we catch Jesus when he's trying to get away for a while. He's out of his own territory in a place where he hopes for a little anonymity. But his reputation has spread and it's impossible to avoid seekers. People in this area were not Jews; therefore, they would have no expectation that Jesus had been sent with a word from Yahweh for them.

This passage actually includes two stories: the account of Jesus with a Syrophoenician woman and the story of Jesus opening the ears and mouth of one who was deaf and mute. These miracles inspired zealous testimonies of Jesus' compassion and power.

But these narratives, especially in relation to each other, offer us clues to Jesus' essential identity and the transformation necessary for his developing ministry.

This is a story of hearing and a story of speaking. It's a story of how both the one who speaks and the one who hears are changed by the speaking and the hearing. It's about the power of speech to evoke change. It's also a story about those things that can silence: xenophobia, nationalism, racism, religious arrogance.

Now this was one disruptive, gutsy woman! Did you hear the tone and demand in her voice? This unnamed woman crossed every line she could cross. She followed in the way of Eve, who dared to act as a free agent, and in the way of Mary, the mother of Jesus, who spoke her vision of a just world that God will bring. Her initiative, her first move, was itself an affront to Jesus. No other woman, especially a Gentile woman who was unrelated to anybody there, would have dared to be so assertive, to invade the privacy of a home to seek a favor.

She was a Canaanite, a woman from the region of Tyre and Sidon, cities whose inhabitants were enemies of Israel. Deep bitterness and hatred separated Jews and Canaanites. Jesus had even warned his disciples to steer clear of Gentiles, reminding them that he and they had been sent only to the lost sheep of the house of Israel.

But Jesus and his followers had forgotten about their boundary-crossing ancestors. You see, Jews were open to others' experiences and identities, and from about 1000 BCE to 600 BCE, the Israelite kingdoms incorporated a variety of non-Israelite communities. Non-Jews were expressly given the equivalent of rights of full citizenship which meant that they fully participated in both secular and religious life. Prophets Zechariah, Jeremiah, and especially Isaiah envisioned peace as a time when many peoples could worship together in the same house, whether or not they were Jewish. But the Jews had forgotten the radical inclusivity that was their heritage. Their self-protective exclusion kept outsiders silent. They stopped their ears with racism, religious arrogance, and sexism.

Let our people (the house of Israel and its tribes), let them be fed first, not the unclean ones, not the Gentile dogs. These are the words of Jesus.

Now, not surprisingly, some biblical scholars have been so

perplexed by the harshness of Jesus' reply that they have tried to tone it down. Some have even gone to great pains to show that the word that Jesus used for dog innocently meant "puppy." Jesus' response really didn't denigrate the woman, they say. Well, whether it means puppy or not, it was clearly a denigrating remark. And, since it's true that early Christian writers emphasized Jesus' divine nature over his humanity, they would never have inserted a scene that brings forward a characteristic as human as prejudice if it had not happened. We can be pretty sure that this is close to an actual event that shaped the life and ministry of Jesus.

Based on who she was (or wasn't) and based on his understanding of who the love of Yahweh was intended for, Jesus tried to silence this desperate woman. But she spoke anyway. Perhaps she knew that if she was going to have any power, any voice, she had to take it rather than wait for it to be granted to her. So, she makes her next move. Her comments are startling and astute. She uses Jesus' rebuke to engage him in a debate:

"Sir, even the dogs under the table eat the children's crumbs."

It is a shocking retort that must have left Jesus astonished. She reached deep inside and found her voice. With the audacity to cross every boundary that would keep her silent, she articulated her need and asserted her right to hope. She stood up for the dignity of her own people, people who were different, those who were outside of the house of Israel. She stood up and claimed their right to the healing power and acceptance of God through Jesus.

When she spoke, the house of cards fell. The lights came on for Jesus, and the system of hierarchy and domination that overshadowed the justice of the prophets was revealed to him. This is the only time in the scriptures that we see Jesus change his mind. This woman speaks and, in her speaking, God's truth of equity is known. And Jesus listens. He could not have seen this coming, and questions must have flooded his mind. Who was he to those outside the fold of Israel? In the larger scheme of things, did he have anything to do with outsiders? Just who was to be included in God's mercy and what might this mean to him and for his ministry?

Because she speaks up with this cogent argument, Jesus tells her that her daughter is already well.

This encounter seems pivotal in defining the scope and character of Jesus' developing ministry. Without the interchange with this audacious woman, Jesus might not have discovered that his mission and God's love were also for those beyond the house of Israel. He might not have learned to listen to those he assumed had no relevance to him.

As Jesus left the region, the gospel writer continues, he encountered a man who could neither speak nor hear. The man's friends begged Jesus to touch him so that he could hear and speak. This encounter seemed to go much more smoothly. Jesus simply took the man aside and opened his ears and voice.

Here's the irony that connects these two stories and shapes the work of Jesus. This man who was deaf and mute wanted to hear and speak. When he approached Jesus, Jesus was fresh from that stinging encounter with the Syrophoenician woman where he had learned the profound importance of speaking and hearing. Because she claimed her voice, Jesus learned the value of speaking – not just physical ability to speak, but finding social and religious voice as well. The one without voice taught Jesus because she was willing and desperate enough to claim this power for herself. Her audacity equipped Jesus to heal others.

Because she talked back, Jesus learned something about how to hear and listen across the lines. Because she talked back, because she took the freedom to speak, assumed that she had the right to

voice her mind, because she spoke in a way that was not determined by her status, she demanded by her boldness that Jesus hear
in a new way. Because of her, Jesus could now freely offer the gift of
speaking *and* the gift of hearing to one who was without.

In offering the gift of speech, was Jesus expressing his willingness to listen? After all, he had his own newfound gift of hearing.
Not only was the woman's need fulfilled and healing brought to
her family, but Jesus, too, found healing of his assumptions about
who could receive the gifts of God and who has the authority to
speak for themselves.

Not only was the one without power transformed when she
dared to speak, but the one with the power was transformed as
well. That's why it's important, men, to listen to the messages of
feminism, not just to treat women more equitably and heal our
wounds, but to heal your own as well. That's why it's important,
white people, to attend to our racism, not just to treat people of
color more equitably and heal their wounds, but to heal our own
as well.

So, Jesus opened the ears of one who could not hear and gave
clarity of voice where speaking was impossible. How important it
was, Jesus knew, to be able to do both.

Jesus put his fingers in the deaf man's ears, and he spat and
touched the man's tongue. Then Jesus looked up to heaven. Now,
listen to what happens next and imagine. Jesus looked up to heaven
– "and he sighed". He sighed. What did he sigh about? What was
he thinking and feeling? I can't help but imagine that he thought
of his Syrophoenician friend as he gave the gift of speaking to this
man. And I suspect that he thought about the gift she had given
him as he made it possible for him to hear.

"He said to the man, 'Be opened!' Immediately his ears were
opened, his tongue was released, and he spoke plainly."

I believe that Jesus speaks these words to us all today: "Ears that have not heard, perhaps that have refused to hear, be opened! Voices that have dared not speak your truth, that have been paralyzed by fear or bullying or simply by cultural expectation of who you are or aren't, speak!" Even when much is at stake, if we dare to find and speak with our own voice, we are changed, our adversaries are changed, and the world is changed.

She spoke; Jesus heard; many witnessed. Exclusion ended in the ministry of Jesus. Power shifted.

Her words became words of life to Jesus and to those who were touched by his boundary-crossing ministry and teaching. I don't think it's overstatement to say that this unnamed woman's voice changed Jesus' entire ministry. He went on to become an egalitarian activist who loved across all the lines that separate people. And he continues to call us to follow that holy way of speaking and listening.

The next time my first response is to silence another, to refuse to listen, I want to look to heaven, breathe a deep sigh, and listen to the one who has dared find their voice. When I look up to heaven, I fully expect to see the ones who learned so much from each other on that day so long ago, there urging us on.

25

THE ONE NOT CHOSEN

Matthew 20:1-16

For the realm of God is like a landowner who went out early in the morning to hire laborers for his vineyard. After agreeing with the laborers for the usual daily wage, he sent them into his vineyard. When he went out about nine o'clock, he saw others standing idle in the marketplace; and he said to them, "You also go into the vineyard, and I will pay you whatever is right." So they went. When he went out again about noon and about three o'clock, he did the same. And about five o'clock he went out and found others standing around; and he said to them, "Why are you standing here idle all day?" They said to him, "Because no one has hired us." He said to them, "You also go into the vineyard." When evening came, the owner of the vineyard said to his manager, "Call the laborers and give them their pay, beginning with the last and then going to the first." When those hired about five o'clock came, each of them received the usual daily wage. Now when the first came, they thought they would receive more; but each of them also received the usual daily wage. And when they received it, they grumbled against the landowner, saying, "These last worked only one hour, and you have made them equal to us who have borne the burden of the day and the scorching heat." But he replied to one of them, "Friend, I am doing you no wrong; did you not agree with me for the usual daily wage? Take what belongs to you and go; I choose to give to this last the same as I give to you. Am I not allowed to do what I choose with what belongs to me? Or are you envious because I am generous?" So the last will be first, and the first will be last.

☙

Our gospel lesson for today is a parable, that is, it's a story with meaning beyond itself, meaning that teases the mind and leaves us with some doubt about what it all means. Jesus' parables were contextual. The culture was agrarian; so, he used agricultural language to make a point about the spiritual world, the world of God and of our higher being. A good preface to a parable might be something like, "If you want life according to God's values, this is how you would live."

Our lesson is from the gospel of Matthew. Now Matthew was an educated writer, writing to an educated Jewish audience. Matthew's readers knew the law. And the law, in Deuteronomy, says this:

> You shall not withhold wages of poor and needy laborers.
> You shall pay them their wages daily before sunset, because
>   they are poor and their livelihood depends on them.
>   (Deuteronomy 24:15)

But Matthew reminds us clearly that this is gospel, not law.

So, we have more than a story about workers in a vineyard, some working longer than others, and the wages they are paid. Like some parables, this one has a surprise turn at the end, a turn which shocks some of the listeners.

Let's look at the story again.

It is grape harvest and the grapes must be gathered or they will ruin on the vines. The vineyard owner needs more hands to get the grapes in; so, as was the labor system of the day, the owner goes to the marketplace at six o'clock in the morning to hire more workers.

The vineyard owner contracts with the workers that are needed, perhaps hiring the fewest number of workers to get the work done and save himself some money. He contracts with them for the normal wage of one denarius for a day's work and they go on their way.

But an hour into the day, the vineyard owner realizes that getting the harvest in is going to take more workers. Concern mounts as the day goes on; so, the owner hires additional workers at nine, then more at noon, at three, and at five, only one hour before the close of the working day.

So far, everything is normal – business as usual. The workers were promised that they would be paid fairly, presumably a portion of a denarius in ratio to the portion of a day.

And then comes pay time. What happens shocks everyone, those who had worked all day and those who were last to be hired. The workers who only worked an hour received a full denarius – the same as those who had worked all day!

Does this part of the story make you cry "injustice"? It does for me. This may be the gospel, but it certainly doesn't seem like good news. Without thinking about it, with whom do you immediately identify? Isn't it interesting that we put ourselves in the place of the ones who have worked all day? I wonder why that is.

The workers who had been there since sunrise felt like they were more deserving than those who had only worked an hour. And perhaps rightly so. But, I think we need to pay attention to how quickly we establish hierarchies of who deserves what – and on what basis we establish them.

Did you notice that the workers who worked all day were treated fairly? They received exactly what they were promised. But they set up a continuum of *worthy* to *unworthy*. Is fairness really the issue that they raise? And it does seem that fairness is the core issue – or should be. The last did not get more than the first, but both received the same. The first workers were okay with one denarius until they saw the gift that was given to those who had worked fewer hours.

Perhaps if good news for others is bad news for us, we could use a change in perspective. Is it possible for the first workers – who were treated fairly – to celebrate with one who has received a generous gift?

As I read this story over and over, trying not to concentrate on what seemed like inequity and trying to find the good news, I realized that some of the characters had been invisible to me. Did you notice them?

The ones who had been waiting, perhaps pleading for work all day in the hot sun, weren't there because they were lazy or didn't want to work, but because no one had hired them.

It could have been something like this:

[Here I take off my pulpit robe, revealing work clothes and a tool belt. I put on a hard hat and move from behind the pulpit to begin a monologue as a contemporary hourly manual laborer.]

It's almost sunrise. I hope it pays to get here early. I lost my regular job when I decided to stay home to care for my neighbor who was sick. She was old and had no one else.

I'm a carpenter by trade, but I'll do anything – any sort of work I can do with my hands. Don't mind hard work. Grapes are ripe and they say the harvest is plentiful this year; so, I hope I can get a couple of days' work bringing in grapes.

Oh, sir, sir! Please, I have debts and...

Perhaps I should knock on doors around the village. Surely someone could use an extra pair of hands.

I don't know what I will do if I can't find a full day's worth of work. My family and my neighbor and her family depend on me so that we can all eat. I can't ask for credit at the market any more. They were so kind when my neighbor took sick – they've done enough.

I really need to be doing something. But what? This is the hard part, standing here waiting and feeling pretty close to helpless.

I guess I could go home. I do have a lot to do at home. But surely someone…

It's getting really late. Even if I started now, I wouldn't make enough to buy food for our evening meal.

What? Can I harvest grapes? Oh, yes. Yes, that will be good.

And so I worked. I worked hard. But for only one hour. I was glad to be chosen finally, but I knew I would earn very little.

And then it happened! You won't believe it! It was as if someone knew exactly what I needed, what I had been waiting for all day. When we were paid, I was given a full day's wages! Can you believe it?

[sings, to the tune of "Beach Spring":]

In my heart, I know I'm chosen
Or my waiting I would end.
Hope of Hope – God of just provision
Saw my need and grace did send.

In God's grace beyond mere justice,
I found a generous source of life
When the one for which I'd waited
Brought a gift of hope and light.

[Here I put my pulpit robe back on to conclude the sermon.]

Through the eyes of one still searching
We can see in different ways.
Find a love that knows our longing,
Sets our waiting hope ablaze.

In God's grace beyond mere justice,
Find a generous source of life,
And the one for which we're waiting
Brings a gift of hope and light.

Through the eyes of the one not chosen until late in the day, we discover a different way of seeing. This helps us locate the good news. Who is deserving? What is fair? What action is generous and life-giving?

The one who was not chosen until late was seeking, eager, willing to work, and waiting to contribute. Who are among those who aren't chosen – by the church and the world? And, if God is the generous vineyard owner, do those who are left out and those who are not invited to serve deserve the equal gifts of God?

We may see those who do not work the whole day as those who seek and seek for God, but faith seems to elude them for years before they find a place of spiritual peace. Or the unchosen ones are those who have been neglected or marginalized by the mainstream church: people of color, sexual minorities, people who are disabled or poor or struggle with mental illness. Or those unchosen may be those who are just different, with personalities or social skills that don't quite fit, or even those who have theological views that are – well – controversial.

For all those who are not chosen by systems or by us, there is a remedy. And it's us. We can change the lack of grace in our lives by applying the truth of this parable from the point of view of the unchosen one who receives an incredible gift.

We can offer gifts of grace like the one offered by the vineyard owner: gifts that are tailor-made for the need that we see in another; gifts that no one has earned – those that we give simply because we see a need and have the means to help. That's what grace is all about.

Have your judgments kept you from offering grace to others in this congregation? Being in community and choosing to offer this sort of grace to each other can be challenging. After all, we know each other's strengths and struggles. And, if we've ever been unchosen ourselves, we may not understand we're fully capable of doing the same to another.

May we learn to see through the eyes of the unchosen one so that we can be freed from jealousy, from comparing our gifts and God's grace toward us with others. May we be freed to receive God's grace and gifts. May we be free, then, to rejoice in God's grace and gifts to others. May we realize that God's justice is never separate from grace! And may we open our hearts and let the grace pour from us.

26

MIND THE GAP

Luke 16:19-31

There was a rich man who was dressed in purple and fine linen and who feasted sumptuously every day. And at his gate lay a poor man named Lazarus, covered with sores, who longed to satisfy his hunger with what fell from the rich man's table; even the dogs would come and lick his sores.

The poor man died and was carried away by the angels to be with Abraham.

The rich man also died and was buried.

In Hades, where he was being tormented, he looked up and saw Abraham far away with Lazarus by his side. He called out, "Father Abraham, have mercy on me, and send Lazarus to dip the tip of his finger in water and cool my tongue; for I am in agony in these flames."

But Abraham said, "Child, remember that during your lifetime you received your good things, and Lazarus in like manner evil things; but now he is comforted here, and you are in agony. Besides all this, between you and us a great chasm has been fixed, so that those who might want to pass from here to you cannot do so, and no one can cross from there to us."

He said, "Then, father, I beg you to send him to my father's house – for I have five brothers – that he may warn them, so that they will not also come into this place of torment." Abraham replied, "They have Moses and the prophets; they should listen to them." He said, "No, father Abraham; but if someone goes to them from the dead, they will repent." He said to him, "If they do not listen to Moses and the prophets, neither will they be convinced even if someone rises from the dead."

☙

IN THE TUBE – the subway – in London, you see signs in many stations cautioning passengers to *Mind the Gap*. The warning, of course, is a call to pay attention to the significant space – the gap – the chasm between the platform and the doorway of the train into which they are about to step. Failure to *Mind the Gap* could result in significant injury and certain embarrassment.

The *gap* – a space between two sides or two things that divides them, separates them from the other. Or, in the case of our gospel story, that which keeps *people* separated from each other – inhabiting different worlds, experiencing life in profoundly different ways.

Now, in the story of the rich man and Lazarus, the gap is a gaping wound, a chilling polarization that divides. Between the two poles stands a veil of pain and fear, a barrier of judgment and self-indulgence that renders "the other" invisible and keeps the self-centered one from knowing his own power to give life.

We recognize those dividing factors, since they also identify modern polarizations: the gate, the lack of motivation to change the status quo, the differences in attire, the need unnoticed, the cuisine.

This is a horrific story.

But I believe that this story is *for* us – *for* the people of God – not against us.

And while it's terribly disturbing, I believe we'd all agree that it's socially predictable. The gap itself. The invisibility. Dehumanizing blindness. We still live with the great chasm, some of us on one side and some of us on the other.

This gap doesn't surprise me one bit. It doesn't surprise me because I have lived in cities: in Atlanta, Minneapolis, Dallas, San Francisco, Tampa, Portland, London. Cities with beautiful high-rise architecture and stately turn-of-one-century-or-another homes, lush parks, trendy restaurants, layers of diversity, and – as predictable as a five-dollar latte – homeless people in various conditions. Panhandlers. Prostitutes. Pitiful, passed-out-from-who-knows-what men and women who don't have the energy to beg. I pass them by; sometimes I see them, sometimes not. What a pity. I often wonder where it all went wrong. But I, like most of us, feel too overwhelmed with the depth and breadth of the problems to even dream of solving them.

Sometimes I hand them a little money. Sometimes I can't bear to look because I know they will connect with something primal inside me and compassion will rise – or fear – or both. So the gap remains. Or, should I say, the *gaps*? With this present recession, new faultlines have emerged, new places of brokenness and economic trouble.

Now, part of me wants to say that this parable isn't just about economics; it's also about greed, destitution, the fortunate and the destitute. And that has its truth: this is also a story about the consequences of arrogance and self-absorption, about theologies that say that God's favor is expressed with economic blessing. It's a story about greed and lack of even the most meager compassion, about being so smug that we don't even see the need right outside our door.

But this parable *is* about economics; it speaks of the responsibilities of compassion, the willingness to be human enough to touch those who have nothing – regardless of what brought about the destitution.

The narrative is in two scenes: the first in the story's present; the second, after both Lazarus and the rich man die. This is a depressing story – the description of the characters graphic and unappealing.

Lazarus was poor, sick, hungry, unnoticed, and expendable; he was motivated only by his desire for enough food to keep himself alive. Surviving by eating the discarded bread that had been used like napkins around the rich man's table was his impetus to remain at the gate. The only attention he received was from the dogs who licked his sores. Jesus gives him a bit of dignity with a name. (Interestingly, Lazarus is the single character in all the parables who is named by Jesus. What might that indicate?)

The rich man had status and wealth: he lived in a gated house, dressed in fine linen and purple, the exquisite color of royalty, and feasted sumptuously daily. In the religious and social structure of the day, those with resources were *expected* to help when others were in desperate need. And yet, the rich man stayed his indulgent course.

The gap was wide.

Assumptions abound in both the story itself and in our contemporary hearing of it: assumptions about righteousness and worthiness that contradict each other and get into a tug-o-war with our faith. In impotence, self-focus, and frustration, we close our eyes to the gap once again, not knowing what to think or do.

Some of us can be so judgmental and self-righteous: "What was it that Lazarus did to end up in his state?" we ask. "If only he hadn't dropped out of school, if only he'd had the willpower to resist that first time someone offered him drugs. What a pity!"

Others have incredible compassion and see him as a powerless victim with no control over his own destiny: as the third generation on the dole, he only knows the culture of poverty. Poor thing. One of those unfortunates who have inherited poverty as surely as they have inherited green eyes or curly hair. He's a victim of who knows how many "isms". As a victim, we may assign him a certain brand of underdog righteousness that stations him closer to God than the rich man.

Perhaps we subscribe to the age-old "health and wealth" theology that convinces us (contrary to the biblical witness) that the one with money is blessed by God. We surely will quickly dismiss this notion and understand the rich man as the oppressor of Lazarus, who is the object of his disdain. After all, the rich man is one who could allow a man to starve to death at his gate.

But lest we tarry too long with any thought that wealth in itself is the culprit, we're assured by the language of the text that wealth also has potential for good. Wealth in itself does not make one either admirable or detestable.

The story tells us that the rich man walked or rode in his chariot past Lazarus daily. He assumed that God was punishing Lazarus for something. But he also must have known the law; he had to remember the words of Deuteronomy that obliged him to "open [his] hand to the poor and needy in the land." (15:11)

Surely, he knew Isaiah's sermon on the fast that God chooses:

Is not [the fast I choose] to share your bread with the hungry, and bring the homeless poor into your house; when you see the naked, to cover them? (58:7)

Mind the Gap is the message of the law and the prophets. "Pay attention to what separates you from others," they preach to us still. Notice. Open your eyes – and act if a chasm divides. Restore what is broken. Re-enfranchise those outside the gate.

In passing Lazarus every day, the rich man disregarded – even opposed – the law of Moses. According to the law, the rich man should have helped Lazarus. But he didn't. In fact, the two never speak to each other. No dialogue. Not even an obligatory nod or the desperate rattling of a tin cup. The scriptures tell us of no acknowledgment or even awareness. The rich man doesn't even bother to have him removed. The gap is wide.

And nothing even changes when the field is leveled by death. Did you notice? Did you hear it? The rich man is still preoccupied with himself, still insulated. He still sees Lazarus as one to provide for his comfort. And Lazarus still doesn't speak; Abraham speaks for him.

In his *Cottonpatch Gospels*, Clarence Jordan stages that dialogue like this:

> The rich man cries out, *Mister Abraham… send Lazarus to dip the end of his finger in some water and rub it over my tongue…*
>
> Abraham answers with the voice of justice: *Lazarus ain't gonna run no mo' yo' errands, rich man.* (Jordan, 318)

Scholars tell us that Jesus probably borrowed a folk tale for this story. That makes sense to me; it could have come from any land at most any time. The poor we always have with us. Where people live, gaps exist – chasms that keep us from knowing or even seeing those who are "other". Gaps divide rich from poor, educated from less educated, employed from unemployed.

The gap divides those who struggle with mental illness from those of us who hold it together most of the time, the able-bodied from those with disabilities. The politically conservative from the politically liberal. Sometimes even men from women, straight from gay, incarcerated from free, undocumented immigrant from citizen, addicted from sober. The Gap.

Moral gaps and social gaps. Human gaps that impoverish all of us and trouble the heart of God.

Oh, we may see stereotypes: we may see "the homeless" – but do we see Lazarus? Joe? Gloria? We may see the problem, but do we see the person? And, further, do we see our part in the person's predicament?

I told you it was a horrific story. But remember: this story is *for* us, not against us.

As people of faith who care about God's creation, we want to Mind the Gap, I believe – to reach across it somehow, to really see each other, give dignity, and treat those in need with compassion; but we don't or can't or don't know how.

The picture is troubling in its similarity. We recognize the scene. The words echo in our minds and spin into reality: "The poor you will always have with you." (Matthew 26:11) Those disturbingly different from you will always be around. Is it enough to know that? Or to have our consciences stirred? Or to toss coins to assuage our guilt?

The gaps are so wide and yet the proximity of those on the other side tugs at our hearts. In the shadow of million-dollar mansions and multi-billion-dollar corporations, people walk with tape holding the last remnant of sole to their shoes.

Let Lazarus represent whatever gap tugs at your heart today. Are you tempted to look away?

Are we doomed to the chasm of alienation – the separation of acceptable from unacceptable? Do we *want* to stay on our side of the gap and continue to pretend we don't see? Or, do we hear the the law and prophets and the words of Jesus: "I was hungry and you gave me food; I was thirsty and you gave me drink." (Matthew 25:35)

Can we see Jesus, see the image of God, when we look across the gap of race or religion or economic destitution?

What might happen – to us and to "Lazarus" – if we did what we could? If we looked into faces instead of diverting our glance? If we engaged in conversation with someone on the other side?

If we can do something to mind the gap, *we* will be changed. We'll look eye-to-eye with our own frailties, our own judgments, our own narrow points of view. We'll discover that the gap isn't quite as wide as we think it is. Perhaps that is actually our main fear. We'll discover our common humanity and tap into our own compassion.

I recently heard about an executive training program. Part of the training was articulating personal values. The trainees were given a hypothetical possibility: that they could eradicate hunger in the world by giving one percent of their income. Then they were asked if they would do it. Not one said they would.

One percent – not a lot. They weren't asked for fifty percent or even ten percent. One percent. Is it as simple as that? Or is it not really about money after all?

It is my prayer that each of us will hear the call to begin minding the gaps that we see around us – for the sake of Lazarus and ourselves, for the sake of the realm of God that is within us and within those across the chasm.

One last thought: with whom did you identify in the story? Some of us may see ourselves as the Lazarus figure. We've been invisible or had our desperate need disregarded in some way. But, at least relatively, most of us probably identify more with the rich man than the totally destitute Lazarus.

But the story has other characters – we may have missed them – the brothers that the rich man left behind. Remember them? We, like they, still have a chance to Mind the Gap, to change things, to make the world a different place, to put a stop to the attitudes and systems that keep us from being fully human. I wonder what we'll do.

27

GETTING IN TROUBLE

Luke 21:5-19

When some were speaking about the temple, how it was adorned with beautiful stones and gifts dedicated to God, he said, "As for these things that you see, the days will come when not one stone will be left upon another; all will be thrown down." They asked him, "Teacher, when will this be, and what will be the sign that this is about to take place?" And he said, "Beware that you are not led astray; for many will come in my name and say, 'I am he!' and, 'The time is near!' Do not go after them. When you hear of wars and insurrections, do not be terrified; for these things must take place first, but the end will not follow immediately." Then he said to them, "Nation will rise against nation, and kingdom against kingdom; there will be great earthquakes, and in various places famines and plagues; and there will be dreadful portents and great signs from heaven. But before all this occurs, they will arrest you and persecute you; they will hand you over to synagogues and prisons, and you will be brought before kings and governors because of my name. This will give you an opportunity to testify. So make up your minds not to prepare your defense in advance; for I will give you words and a wisdom that none of your opponents will be able to withstand or contradict. You will be betrayed even by parents and brothers, by relatives and friends; and they will put some of you to death. You will be hated by all because of my name. But not a hair of your head will perish. By your endurance you will gain your souls."

❧

I'M GOING TO paraphrase and contemporize our gospel lesson for today:

When some were speaking about our church building, how it was adorned with beautiful stained glass and furnishings dedicated to God, Jesus said, "As for these things that you see, the days will come when not one brick will be left upon another; all will be torn down."

Then we ask him, "Teacher, when will this be, who will tear down our building and what will be the sign that this is about to take place?"

Jesus says, "You've been listening to those television preachers again, haven't you? They tell you that wars and starvation and even – well, you know – the homosexual agenda, and unusual occurrences in weather and disease are all signs of the end of the earth. But all of this – except maybe that imaginary agenda – has been around the whole time! Somehow it's easier to predict and look into the future than it is to live in the present.

"I think I need to tell you again about following me, believing that grace is for all – that sin is really about not loving and passing that grace on. A spiritual life is about turning the other cheek, offering love in the face of hatred, working for justice and peace, treating all people as God's Beloved. Do you know what that means?

"Bringing in this New Age is not very popular. People like to create hierarchies of holiness – you know – the 'I'm in, you're not' game. So if you work for justice and treat others with grace, if you give yourself to righteousness and equality, they may arrest you and persecute you; they may send you to prison and bring you to trial because you want to upset their applecart.

"This will give you an incredible opportunity! You can speak of the freedom to be fully human that you have found, of the grace and power, of the lifting of shame and the joining of my spirit with yours. Think of it! I will give you wisdom and words – you will be powerful as you tell of God's love for you and for your enemies alike.

"Your enemies may be able to overtake you by force or by law, but they can't match your love and your openness. Vulnerability can be so much stronger than force. I know it sounds harsh, but many of you know that even parents and brothers and sisters, relatives and friends will turn away; some of you may even die for our way of life. As amazing as it seems, you will be hated because of my name.

"But, I promise you this: When you lose your life in this way, you save it. By your faithfulness, you will gain your souls."

In this lesson from Luke, Jesus was calling his followers into the present, away from speculations about the end times. He was calling them to be the body of Christ in the present, to live as Jesus did – in the here and now. This is a dangerous thing. It was dangerous for Jesus. Clearly, it was dangerous for the twelve. The lions in the amphitheatres were the fate of many early Christians in the Roman Empire as they challenged the role of government and the place of God.

And following in the ways of Jesus – in loving defiance of many of our world's values – has been dangerous in the world after Jesus as well. We know some stories of other Christians, their challenges to status-quo power, how they were demonized or humored or set aside as different by those powers, and we know of their persecutions.

We know about Joan of Arc, and those persecuted as witches at Salem, Massachusetts. We know about Martin Luther King, Jr., and those nameless Christians who protected their Jewish brothers and sisters from Nazi annihilation. We know what happened when they tried to protect the lives and dignity of those who were second class or third class or no class, those who were feared or hated.

We know of Mother Teresa – sainted, set apart, as though no one else could love and serve so selflessly and wholeheartedly. When we assign this character to only a few, we imply that the ways of Jesus are beyond the reach of all of us. We might also recall Dorothy Day who valued those considered disposable. Or Frances Willard who, in the late nineteenth century, dared to propose that women were equal to serve the church. Never heard of her? What a surprise!

We get in trouble with the powers that be – even the church, my friends – when we dare to propose that *all* of us are God's beloved. We get into trouble when we want to give those on whom our world has given up an extra break, when we upset the structures of haves and have-nots.

We get into trouble when we speak up for justice and when we dare to connect justice for all with the name of Jesus. We get ourselves into trouble when we open this Eucharistic table to all, when we refuse to be judge and jury about who's holy enough. We run in the danger zone when we stop being victimized minorities and begin to be the church in the wider community. We place ourselves in the firing line when we dare suggest that the pulpit as well as the pew, the table as well as the confessional, and most of all the lap of Jesus, are places for gay, immigrant, and at-risk youth.

We even get into trouble with the Christian establishment when we suggest that perhaps the issue is not who is allowed at this table but rather that we can come here morally and spiritually bankrupt and find life; when we refuse to take the words of scripture out of context – including the context of our lives and the work of the Spirit in us; when we believe with our words and our actions that healing is the mission of the church and work for reconciliation at very high cost.

I contemporized our lesson for today because I believe that this text is for us. We must hear the words of Jesus as a call to us. Are we prepared to be the church in our world? Do we have the courage to live as Jesus lived – equipped with the spirit and our own passion for justice? Is it worth the risk of getting into trouble?

Even if we know that abundant life – real purposeful living – is the result, we must have courage if we are to bring in God's new age that Jesus began. Courage is, indeed, the chief virtue. Without it, other virtues are non-functional. We can either keep this new age of love, justice, and peace in the safety of our sanctuaries, or we can risk changing the world around us. We can either decide that faith has to do only with private devotion to God, that religion is a Sunday morning, "don't take it outside and get it dirty" proposition, debating how soon the world will end and how the realm of God will come, counting wars and days and signs in the sky, or we can be those who bring about that realm of God every day, risking whatever we feel God is calling us to risk, to tell the truth and do the right thing, to bring the spirit of healing and do the work of reconciliation.

We can either play it safe or trust in the leading of the spirit and the wisdom of God. We can ponder the grace we've received and give thanks for it and stop at that, or we can proclaim and live and pass that grace along, and watch our own faith break the dam of fear and gush forth in springs of living water for a thirsty world.

Is there promise with this risk? Absolutely! The promise is always the presence of God. The promise is divine wisdom and a relevant faith. And the promise is that we have the incredible privilege of being partners with Jesus in changing the world – if we're willing to get into trouble as well.

Jesus describes an amazing paradox: a blessed opportunity to get into trouble, a sweet burden, a joyous risk, a desirable trauma, a cherished cross. If we dare speak the truth, care enough to heal, touch the untouchable, speak names unutterable; the blessing awaits us.

May it be so.

28

DO JUSTICE

Amos 5:21-24

I hate, I despise your festivals, and I take no delight in your solemn assemblies. Even though you offer me your burnt offerings and grain offerings, I will not accept them; and the offerings of well-being of your fatted animals I will not look upon. Take away from me the noise of your songs; I will not listen to the melody of your harps. But let justice roll down like waters, and righteousness like an everflowing stream.

ॐ

This sermon was given in Birmingham, England, on Remembrance Sunday 2008.

ॐ

"AN EYE FOR an eye and a tooth for a tooth, and," says Tevye in the musical *Fiddler on the Roof,* "all the world would be blind and toothless." (Stein)

More often than not, "justice" is understood as enforcement of law. This may have been the notion of justice derived from the Pentateuch, but the Hebrew prophets had something quite different to say.

Proclaiming what it meant to be the people of Yahweh in their time, the voices of Jeremiah and Micah and Amos ring out, calling the people of God to a brand of justice infused with compassion. They speak clear words about the imperative values and way of life for people of God: the ethic and life of justice, compassion, and truth. They cut to the quick of hypocrisy, and yet offer the hope that is God's sense of rightness.

"Let justice roll down like waters, and righteousness like an ever-flowing stream," pleads the prophet Amos as he speaks for God.

We use this word with ease in our own minority communities: *justice*. It's a byword, a call to action, a demand for our voices to be heard.

Over two thousand verses of Scripture equate justice with standing up for *the poor*, feeding *the poor*, bringing justice to *the poor*. Doing justice and righteousness is the same thing as taking up the cause of the poor, standing with those who are oppressed, speaking on behalf of those who have no voice – until they find their voices and speak for themselves.

The writer of Proverbs assures us that "if we indeed cry out for insight, and raise our voices for understanding; then we will understand righteousness and justice and equity, every good path." (Proverbs 2:3-5)

The prophets call us to "wash ourselves; make ourselves clean; cease to do evil, learn to do good; seek justice, rescue the oppressed, defend the orphan, plead for the widow." (Isaiah 1:16-17)

The prophet Isaiah exhorts:

Give counsel, grant justice;
make your shade like night at the height of noon;
hide the outcasts, do not betray the fugitive;
let the outcasts of Moab settle among you; be a refuge to them
from the destroyer. (Isaiah 16:3-4)

In the meta-narrative of Exodus – the long journey from slavery to freedom – the voice of God says to Moses: "I will send you to Pharaoh to bring my people out of Egypt." (Exodus 3:10)

Amos was a prophet at the height of Israel's power and influence. The nation was at peace, the religious leaders were favored by the king. Israel's leaders were prosperous, but this prosperity came at a price. There was a downtrodden underclass – the poor. They were overtaxed. Their land was seized. Widows were begging in the streets. Israel had been guided by God to be a model culture: to take care of the poor, the sick, the widows and the orphans. But the Israelites were failing to do these things.

Instead of attending to basic human need as the way to follow Yahweh, they substituted scrupulous religiosity and forgot how to live. They attended to the rituals of their faith – brilliant worship and music. Now, there's nothing wrong with inspiring worship and beautiful music, but it's not an instead-of proposition.

Here's what Amos, as an oracle of God, says of them:

They sell the righteous for silver and the needy for a pair of sandals. They push the afflicted out of the way. (Amos 2:6b-7a)

In the house of God, they drink wine bought with fines they imposed. (Amos 2: 6b-8b)

But let justice roll down like waters. Justice, not sacrifice. Justice, *mishpat* in Hebrew, doesn't mean that the good are rewarded, and the bad are punished. It literally means that the neediest are cared for. The worship of Israel was wrong not exactly because it was idolatrous. It was wrong because the worshipers were not living with righteousness and justice.

Theologian Dorothee Soelle asserts that theology without an economic thread is antithetical to biblical theology. She writes:

God's message is unambiguous: "You are to feed the hungry, clothe the naked, bury the dead, visit the imprisoned." All of the works are "forbidden" by the economic structure in which we live. It is designed to let the hungry starve, make the rich richer and the poor poorer. (Soelle, *Against the Wind*, 99)

What is now a worldwide system of thought and actions began in Latin America with the one that Henri Nouwen simply calls "a little man from Peru." (Nouwen, *!Gracias!*, 144-145) He was Gustavo Gutierrez, a man without power, living in a *barrio* with poor people, who wrote a book entitled *A Theology of Liberation* that has been considered dangerous by political leaders.

In this book, Gutierrez, whose work laid the foundation for modern liberationist movements, reclaimed the truth of the prophets and Jesus: that God's desire is to bring good news to the poor and liberty to the captives – *literally, politically, economically*. With the voice of Amos, Gutierrez calls for action, for economic and political equity for all.

This sort of justice – if we were to really do it – has the power to remake our world. It threatens our privileges, it demands change in our social structures. This sort of justice sees the dignity of every child of God, and acts to protect and promote that dignity, *even when it costs us*. But to risk our privileges and our comfort is to meet God anew.

Situations that cry out for God's justice surround and overwhelm us: the reign of terror in Zimbabwe, murders of lesbians and refugees in South Africa, inhumane treatment of prisoners of war, the growing underclass in most of the world.

Here in Britain, this is Remembrance Sunday. We remember those from every nation who have died in times of war. In 1980, Remembrance Sunday was broadened to extend the re-membrance to all who have suffered and died in conflict in the service of their country and all those who mourn them.

We do mourn those lost and those who suffer in any way because of the horrors of war. *And*, as we examine the biblical concepts of justice, we work and pray for the day when no more lives will be lost in the political and economic conflicts that plague our world. Our world cries out for the sort of justice/love to which the prophets call us!

The global injustices we see could overwhelm us, but the point of this sermon is not to have you feel guilty for not doing enough. Rather, the point is to give us a glimpse of the rolling river of justice that reveals to us more fully the realm of God – God's love and peace – and to tempt us into doing justice right where we are, so that God can be known, beginning with us.

Let me illustrate this with an example from a friend and ministry colleague. George is a young African minister who was a pastor in an evangelical denomination. When George began to realize that he was a gay man, he began to learn the nature of a God of justice and the violations of the church. He noticed that gay folks weren't the only ones who had church doors slammed in their faces. The church also rejected those who were poor and ill. George heard the call of God to do justice, to let it rush like a mighty river.

He preached the inclusive love of God and the biblical imperative of justice on the streets of his town, calling the church to care for those on the margins. The result was that, at the hands of the church, he was arrested and taken to jail. Despite the abuses he suffered there, the call was clear and he refused to be silenced. Who was left out? Who did the church exclude from singing their hymns of praise? George concluded that that's exactly who the church needs to reach and include – and his church does. In fact, it's comprised of those who aren't welcomed elsewhere.

There, in the faces of those outcast, God is known. In the worship that flows from justice and gratitude, the Spirit moves.

That's the point. It's Amos's point. And it's the point of Jesus, I believe. It's this: in doing justice, in showing compassion and kindness – even when it costs us – in meeting and knowing those on the margins, God is known and worshiped and the world is, at least in those moments, put right.

You see, when we think for a moment that being Christian is getting ready for the next world, we've missed the message of the prophets and of Jesus. Jesus didn't come to get us ready for the next world; he came into this world to transform us into people in whom God could be known.

In his legendary "I Have a Dream" speech, Martin Luther King, Jr. wove our text for today into his vision for racial justice: "… until justice rolls down like waters and righteousness like a mighty stream." He used virtually the same paraphrase of Amos throughout his career. (Amos 5:24)

Several years ago, I visited the Montgomery, Alabama, monument to Dr. King at the Southern Poverty Law Center. The memorial is a monumental sweep of concrete with water sheeting across the façade. Engraved on the face of the stone are the words: "Let justice roll down like waters and righteousness like an ever-flowing stream."

But I noticed something odd: the quotation was credited to Martin Luther King, Jr., not to the prophet Amos. I assumed it was an embarrassing mistake, but then I reflected on that error. These words of the prophet had become so alive in the justice-doing of this man and this movement that they had become the very word of God for another time and another action. These were no longer only *historic* words of God, but the *alive* and powerful word of God, inspiring and invoking God's love and justice.

How can we become the justice that rolls down to put our world right?

We can do justice in small ways. Even if we put aside one coin per day for a justice cause, and with it prayed for justice, it would make a difference and make us better disciples as well. Or write something that promotes justice. When you're moved to do something and you don't know what to do, write a letter to your Member of Parliament, a note to a friend, a blog, a sermon, a supportive letter to someone suffering.

Anything. Just do something to promote justice.

Choose a fair-trade product – just once and even if it costs more. And pray for those who are exploited for economic greed. Even if each of us only does this once, something will change.

Challenge one unjust attitude in yourself: how you spend your money, lingering racism or sexism, classism or ableism. Look a homeless person directly in the eyes and speak. Then, bring what you've done with you to the worship of God. Connect the dots of love and justice and the presence of God.

Do you want to encounter God? Do justice!

Do you want to experience life in all its fullness? Do justice!

Do you want your worship to be filled with power and hope? Do justice!

Do you want your life to make a difference in the world? Do justice!

Do you want to be a disciple of Jesus? Do justice!

29

THE NAMES LIVE ON
All Saints Day

Sirach 44:1-15

Let us now sing the praises of our ancestors in their generations. God appointed to them great glory and majesty from the beginning. There were those who ruled in their kingdoms and made a name for themselves by their valor; those who gave counsel because they were intelligent; those who spoke in prophetic oracles; those who led the people by their counsels and by their knowledge of the people's lore; they were wise in their words of instruction; those who composed musical tunes, or put verses in writing; those endowed with resources living peacefully in their homes – all these were honored in their generations, and were the pride of their times. Some of them have left behind a name, so that others declare their praise. But of others there is no memory; they have perished as though they had never existed; they have become as though they had never been born, they and their children after them. But these also were godly, whose righteous deeds have not been forgotten; their wealth will remain with their descendants, and their inheritance with their children's children. Their descendants stand by the covenants; their children also, for their sake. Their offspring will continue forever, and their glory will never be blotted out. Their bodies are buried in peace, but their names live on generation after generation. The assembly declares their wisdom, and the congregation proclaims their praise.

Revelation 7:9-17

After this I looked, and there was a great multitude that no one could count, from every nation, from all tribes and peoples and languages, standing before the throne and before the Lamb, robed in white, with palm branches in their hands. They cried out in a loud voice, saying, "Salvation belongs to our God who is seated on the throne, and to the Lamb!" And all the angels stood around the throne and around the elders and the four living creatures, and they fell on their faces before the throne and worshiped God, singing, "Amen! Blessing and glory and wisdom and thanksgiving and honor and power and might be to God forever and ever! Amen."

Then one of the elders addressed me, saying, "Who are these, robed in white, and where have they come from?" I said to him, "Sir, you are the one that knows." Then he said to me, "These are they who have come out of the great ordeal; they have washed their robes and made them white in the blood of the Lamb. For this reason they are before the throne of God, and worship God day and night within the temple, and the one who is seated on the throne will shelter them. They will hunger no more, and thirst no more; the sun will not strike them, nor any scorching heat; for the Lamb at the center of the throne will be their shepherd, and he will guide them to springs of the water of life, and God will wipe away every tear from their eyes."

℃℈

THE CHURCH CELEBRATES All Saints Sunday as a time of remembrance, an occasion to acknowledge and experience the presence of those who have gone before. While this day is somewhat somber, it's also a celebration. In this day is both painful parting and promising hope.

My earliest recollections of funerals were those I chose not to attend. They were services for older people in the church that I didn't know well. During the days before each of several funerals, my parents told me about the deaths and gave me the option to go to the funeral – or not. I chose not. I chose not repeatedly, to the point of developing quite a bit of resistance to the idea of going to funerals.

Then, my senior year at university, the wife of one of my favorite professors died. He invited me to sing in the choir at her funeral. I couldn't refuse. It turned out to be the best possible first funeral experience for me. It was a high Anglican service, using the Easter liturgy directly from the prayer book, just as if it were the Day of Resurrection. Right in the middle of the grief and loss came assuring, even joyous, words and soaring Hallelujahs!

This is such a day. Losses remembered with the light of eternity slipping into the shadows of our grief.

All Saints Day is about remembering, naming, reflecting on how we are formed by those gone before.

About life and death and hope and legacy.

And it's about the communion of saints, that experience of being surrounded by the great cloud of witnesses. About being joined on the journey by those mostly unseen ancestors who inspire and guide us by their lives that shaped us and, perhaps for some, their spirits that stay with us still.

On this All Saints Sunday, we remember and celebrate those who have gone before us in the faith, those who helped us find our own faith, who modeled the love of God, who molded our values and character by their very lives.

As in the Orthodox Church where the sanctuary is surrounded by icons of the saints, I would propose that we, too, worship today with those who have died. With the writer of Revelation, we glimpse through the veil of heaven and earth – life and death – where we see scores of saints from every nation and every tribe!

Who do you see there as we open the eyes of our hearts to join the writer in peering through that veil?

Who are saints? They are those who traverse the difficulties of life and still allow hope to guide them; those who look to God and serve others; those through whom and in whom the Spirit stays alive in the world. Saints are those whose love and hope and vitality and perseverance guide us still.

Ernest J. Gaines, acclaimed author of *The Autobiography of Miss Jane Pittman* and *A Lesson Before Dying*, takes care of an old cemetery on the former plantation where five generations of his ancestors, going back to slavery, are buried. Interviewed for a newspaper article, he talks about why he does this:

> If I didn't have those people back there, I would never have had anything to write about. That's where I got all my stories from. My life is from them... I'm going to do everything to keep up for them, in memory. That is my duty. (Seelye)

A number of storytellers offer versions of this same beautiful little story, the story of a little girl who has invited a friend to church. As they're sitting with the child's father waiting for the service to begin, the young visitor asks her friend who the people are in the stained-glass windows. Relaying what her parents have taught her, she tells her friend that those people are saints.

"Who are saints?" her friend asks.

As if it answered everything, the little girl replies, "Saints are the people the light shines through."

Indeed! Saints are those through whom the Light shines, through whom God is known and the world is made better. They are those in whom holiness is something quite different than being without fault; it is goodness and light and wonder and hope and love-in-action.

Who are saints?

The Catholic Church declares specific people saints through stringent examination and clear criteria, criteria like performing miracles and healing physical maladies, leading exemplary lives, focused on others. Oh – and they have to be dead!

The Catholic Church teaches that it does not, in fact, *make* anyone a saint. Rather, it *recognizes* a saint.

Who are saints?

We might agree that there are many more people the light shines through than the church recognizes. And many, I know, fill our hearts.

This passage from Sirach is one of my favorites in all the scriptures. It's from one of the apocryphal books of the Bible – a book of Wisdom literature. I was introduced to the passage about fifteen years ago when I was invited to preach at the Pride Service for Integrity, the LGBT Episcopal organization, in Atlanta. Now the Atlanta Pride theme that year was Generations of Pride. What? Feeling pride about being a gay or lesbian, bisexual, or transgender person is a new thing – we surely can't look to previous generations for examples of out and proud gay men or lesbians!

Well, the Integrity leaders had brilliantly chosen this passage as the focus of their service. The passage basically says that some have gone before us who have done great things, and we have monuments that testify to their greatness. Others have also gone before who have changed us and changed the world for good, but their names are not well known. But we know them and our lives are living monuments to their legacies. They live on through those who remember them.

We know these people, don't we? They've inspired us and given us direction and hope. Saints!

A lovely hymn was written by Lesbia Scott and included in her book *Everyday Hymns for Little Children*.

> I sing a song of the saints of God….
> You can meet them in school, or in lanes, or at sea,
> In church, or in trains, or in shops, or at tea!

In a jolly way, she reveals them to us, helps us see that they are all around us, letting the light of God shine through them.

What if we regarded those in whom we see the light as saints of God? How might our view and treatment of each other change if we saw those around us as saints? We might ask them questions about who they are, who God is to them, about the principles by which they live. We would want to be with them, absorb what gives them life.

It's easy to make saints of dead people. They don't have disagreements or make mistakes. Their rough edges get sanded away by time and legend. Those "sainted" by the church are to some degree idealized, sanitized, frozen in time.

What about God's saints today? Who is it that bears God's touch and heart to us? Can we recognize the light shining through those closest to us? Can we see God in our very human friends and even our families? How might we, they, our community be changed if we were to "saint" one another with our honor, respect, attention? How might we – and this community – be better if we began to recognize the light shining through those around us? How might we be better if we – like the church – recognized God's power and presence in the self-giving, in the wisdom, in the God-seeking, in the justice-pressing activism, in the compassion poured out by those we know and love?

In the Southern Baptist Church in which I grew up, some of the older adults called each other Brother and Sister. It was more than a term of endearment or even respect. It was somehow recognizing their place in the faith, seeing their contribution to the people of God and the way their faith both shaped their own lives and touched others. Perhaps they were, in a Southern way, sainting each other.

What light we could see, what wisdom we could discover if we found the saints among us: if we had Saint Harry or Saint Angela, Saint Billy or Saint Barbara.

You see it, don't you? You see the gifts of these saints of God: the wisdom, the ability to move through the difficulties of life, to forgive and let others be human. You see the kindness and sweet-spiritedness and deep strength of the saints among us. They bring to us the insight to know what matters and why, their mindful living and their constant concern for others and the world.

If we're going to see the saints among us, there's a bit of a danger that someone might just look at us as saints, too, isn't there? We run the risk that someone might see the light of God shining through us.

Most of us would resist that notion, wouldn't we? So would many of the people who have been canonized as saints by the Catholic Church. After people have died, we get a different perspective on them and how they lived their lives. Some of those honoured as saints would have been branded heretics during their lifetimes. We, too, resist that designation for ourselves.

And yet, that's what happens when we open our lives to the love and wisdom and compassion of Christ, when we traverse life's challenges with steadfast hope and prevailing love. Our lives, too, inspire and guide.

The last phrase of Lesbia Scott's children's hymn makes this crucial statement:

For the saints of God are just folk like me, and I mean to be one too.
… and there's not any reason, no, not the least, why I shouldn't be one too.

Truth is – we're all both sinners and saints, even those who bear special titles. That's important to remember, to know at our heart.

It keeps us real and humble and clear. Most of us would 'fess up to the sinner part. But we need to know that we're saints as well.

Today, we remember those gone before us. We take in their essence and live their legacy. We honour them and their light and lives. We also open our eyes to the saints around us, to avail ourselves of their wisdom and inspiration.

And, perhaps, we can live our lives, too, knowing that God's life is in us all. We can all be saints of God – looking for places to shine our light, letting compassion outshine self-pity, finding opportunities to serve others, reaching deep for God in times of trouble, taking every opportunity to love, to be kind, to offer ourselves in service.

May it be so, saints of God.

30

OUT ON A LIMB

Luke 19:1-10

Jesus entered Jericho and was passing through it. A man was there named Zacchaeus; he was a chief tax collector and was rich. He was trying to see who Jesus was, but on account of the crowd he could not, because he was short in stature. So he ran ahead and climbed a sycamore tree to see him, because he was going to pass that way. When Jesus came to the place, he looked up and said to him, "Zacchaeus, hurry and come down; for I must stay at your house today." So he hurried down and was happy to welcome him. All who saw it began to grumble and said, "He has gone to be the guest of one who is a sinner." Zacchaeus stood there and said to Jesus, "Look, half of my possessions I will give to the poor; and if I have defrauded anyone of anything, I will pay back four times as much." Then Jesus said to him, "Today salvation has come to this house, because he too is a son of Abraham. For the Son of God came to seek out and to save the lost."

❧

MY EXPERIENCE IS that much of life's anxiety comes from either feeling guilty or feeling offended.

Think about it. When we're out of sorts, we may feel filled with shame for something we've done or something we've failed to do, or we feel hurt or angry because of what someone else has done to us. We're perpetrator or victim, oppressor or oppressed, offender or offended. How often our psyches put us at one extreme or the other!

I once heard someone articulate it like this: "I'm either *it* or I'm… [something that rhymes with 'it']." I'm either above others or scraping the bottom of life's barrel.

Our gospel lesson today is one of those stories that many of us remember from childhood Sunday School. Because we tend to remember that wee little man and the tree-climbing adventure, we may have missed that this is a story about very real and relevant aspects of our human struggle.

We may have missed that Zacchaeus was demonized by many or that Jesus stepped into a politically risky situation and took that risk for the sake of what often seems unlikely: a greedy, dishonest person can change his ways. Perhaps we overlook Zacchaeus's dramatic turn of heart that challenged him to perform a difficult series of actions – going out on a limb in more ways than one. Because we assume that Zacchaeus is the outcast, we may not have noticed that the bystanders had that victim mentality, standing in non-reflective judgment on the one who had done them wrong.

This is a story about grudges held, about making amends, and seeking to make things right.

Zacchaeus was ready to see Jesus. And Jesus knew it. It may be that Zacchaeus's guilt was consuming him. He couldn't even venture into the marketplace without getting a glimpse of someone whose misery was his fault. Guilt can occupy our nightmares and make up things to avoid during the daylight.

Zacchaeus may have been longing for a way to turn his life around, to look his neighbors in the eye once again, to regain self-respect and dignity.

Can we feel his desperation? I suspect that most of us feel guilt

– genuine guilt, not the guilt-trip kind – about something. Are we so tired of our own unresolved issues, those things that we hope will go away, that we'll go out on a metaphorical limb to find relief? Are we ready to move on?

A sign in front of a church said, "If you're done with sin, come on in." But, underneath that clever rhyme, someone had printed in lipstick: "If you're not quite through, call 555-1332."

The truth is that we may not be done with our guilt yet. So we carry a heavy load that torments us. But when we're ready to go out on a limb, ready to make it right, we can find a way in the Zacchaeus story.

Rather than joining sides with those who wanted Zacchaeus to know what a bad guy everyone knew he was, Jesus actually sought him out and invited himself into the tax collector's life. Jesus looked him in the eye, sat at the dinner table with him, actually – imagine it – treated him like he was a good person!

But Zacchaeus isn't the only character in the story who needs relief. Those who observed the whole Zacchaeus-and-Jesus scene had plenty to say about it. They had probably been victims of Zach's tax extortion scheme. They knew first-hand that people like Zacchaeus were just out for themselves. They were – everyone knew – beyond redemption. Unclean. Unethical. Unreachable. Perhaps being up a tree was symbolic.

They didn't like greedy, thieving tax officials or the oppressive system itself, and – quite frankly – they were appalled that Jesus was wasting time with such a scoundrel. Those bystanders resented Zacchaeus and all he represented. And they surely resented Jesus' attention to him.

Got resentment? It's that feeling of indignant displeasure, persistent ill-will, clear pain and anger from being wronged, insulted, injured. I *can't* let her off the hook after what she did.

And so I hold on. She may never know, but resentment consumes me.

Resentment is the result of holding onto our injury day after day, year after year. When we ignore it, or let it get a foothold, it grows into feelings of hate or acts of revenge.

According to Nietzsche, nothing "consumes a [person] more completely than the passion of resentment." (Nietzsche, 21)

Resentment is a sign of spiritual disturbance. If we harbor resentment, something is out of kilter. We're holding on to injury, nursing our hurt, justifying our self-righteousness. And it can only get worse. Resentments keep us negative, victimized, arrogant, judgmental, or defeated.

We prefer retaliation. It's true. We hold on to the anger, resentment, sense of betrayal and bitterness until it consumes us or makes our lives unbearable. But it feels good and right in the beginning. By putting someone else – the offender – in a despised spot, I put myself on a pedestal.

Jesus makes an interesting connection in the prayer that we know as The Lord's Prayer.

This is from one translation of the Aramaic text of that prayer:

Loose the cords of mistakes that bind us
As we release the strands we hold of others' guilt. (Klotz, 30)

Our own release is intertwined with our ability to release others. The forgiveness we need has a hard time breaking through our thick defenses, fears, and blaming. We can't see a way forward. Or it's just too hard. Fear consumes us.

But Zacchaeus just did it. He took a chance, went out on a limb. And he broke through. Jesus paid attention to him, didn't turn away for a moment. And, ready to make his life right, Zacchaeus absorbed the grace and took another step. He made amends. And he did it with humility, offering more than was required for restitution.

Might that work for us?

In the Twelve Steps of Alcoholics Anonymous, those who adopt the program as a way of life are urged to "head straight for the person concerned and lay their cards on the table":

> We needn't wallow in excessive remorse before those we have harmed, but amends at this level should always be forthright and generous.
>
> Above all, we should try and be absolutely sure that we are not delaying because we are afraid. For the readiness to take the full consequences of our past acts, and to take responsibility for the well-being of others at the same time, is the very spirit of [… making amends]. (*Twelve Steps*, 85-87)

Several weeks ago, after a short homily that I gave during a meeting here at the church, a woman I didn't know pulled me aside and said that she needed to make something right with me. She began to tell me that she had not only believed rumors about me that she now knew weren't true, but further, she had maliciously spread those rumors. She said that she intended to set the record straight and offered this amends with tears and sorrow.

After my initial shock, I, of course, thanked her for her confession and accepted her apology. On reflection, what troubled me was that she was clearly in deep despair about something that I knew absolutely nothing about, something that had happened nearly a decade previously. It could've been resolved so easily, and yet fear or shame kept her from peace.

So, this is a call to action – for each of us – to take care of our guilt, our resentments, to make it right. We do this for both our own inner peace and so that we can live in right and good relationship with God and each other.

Something happens in this story that is beyond Zacchaeus, beyond someone making amends for what he's done, even beyond the power of personal transformation. Zacchaeus recognizes an obligation to eliminate abuses in the tax system itself, encouraging more honesty, transparency, and even restitution to those harmed. He seems to know that his future, his peace depends on willingness to go out on a limb and make it right. And we can imagine that the whole town is changed. A dent is made in a corrupt tax system. Cynics see that there may yet be hope for corrupt political systems. Poor people may feel for the first time that they have a chance.

While our amends may not make such drastic and far-reaching political and economic impact, our actions of grace and gratitude – of taking responsibility and risking honesty – are powerful and the impact will be felt way beyond ourselves.

Humility and grace are multiplied when we act them out in the world, when we dare to believe that, with God's love and favor, we can be truthful and repentant.

Jesus pronounced salvation on Zacchaeus's house, healing and hope. Wherever honesty and confession and amends abide, and wherever humility surrenders to arrogance and resentment, salvation is known. Shalom. Abundant life.

May we take it on ourselves to do that saving work – for ourselves and the sake of the world.

Bibliography

Adler, Jerry. "In Search of the Spiritual." *Newsweek,* 5 September 2005.

Augustine of Hippo. Sermon 263A: "On the Ascension of the Lord." 396-397.

Barth, Karl. Cited in Kenneth Leech. *True Prayer.* San Francisco: Harper & Row, 1980.

Bernier, Larry. "Our God Is Like an Eagle." *The Hymnal Project.* San Francisco: MCC San Francisco, 1980.

Billington, James H. *Russia in Search of Itself.* New York: Woodrow Wilson Center, 2004.

Borg, Marcus J. *The Heart of Christianity: Rediscovering a Life of Faith.* New York: HarperCollins, 2003.

Bornstein, Kate. *Gender Outlaw: On Men, Women, and the Rest of Us.* New York: Routledge, 1994.

Bowie, Walter Russell. "O Holy City, Seen of John." 1910. *The New Century Hymnal.* Cleveland: Pilgrim, 1995.

Brown, Dan. *The Da Vinci Code.* New York: Random House, 2003.

Brown, Robert McAfee. *Unexpected News: Reading the Bible with Third World Eyes.* Philadelphia: Westminster, 1984.

Carr, Adrienne and John. *We Are an Easter People: The Triumph of God's Love in Our Lives: Leader's Guide.* Nashville: Upper Room, 1990.

Chapman, Tracy. "Change." *Where You Live.* Atlantic, 2005. CD.

Chaput, Charles J. "Faith and Patriotism." *New York Times,* 22 October 2004.

Coen, Joel. *O Brother, Where Art Thou?* Burbank: Touchstone Pictures, 2000. DVD.

Complete Jewish Bible, The. Ed. David H. Stern. Dordrecht: Importantia, 2006.

Corrington, Gail Paterson. *Her Image of Salvation: Female Saviors and Formative Christianity.* Louisville: Westminster John Knox, 1992.

Covey, Stephen R. *The Seven Habits of Highly Effective People: Powerful Lessons in Personal Change.* New York: Simon and Schuster, 1989.

Cowman, Mrs. Charles. *Streams in the Desert.* Cowman, 1928.

"Dem Bones." Traditional spiritual.

Disciples of Christ theologian. Community Christian Church (Disciples). Web. 2006.

Ebb, Fred. "Married." *Cabaret.* New York: Alley Music / Trio Music, 1966.

Emerson, Ralph Waldo. "Miracles: An Address Delivered before the Senior Class in Divinity College." Boston, 1838. Keynote address.

France, R. T. *The Gospel of Matthew.* Grand Rapids: Eerdmans, 2007.

Frost, Robert. "The Road Not Taken.*" Mountain Interval.* New York: Henry Holt, 1920.

Geriatric Mental Health Foundation. "Late Life Depression: A Fact Sheet." Web. 2014.

Gillard, Richard. "Servant Song." *Scripture in Song.* Maranatha Music, 1977.

Goodstein, Laurie. "Order Dismisses a Priest Trying to Ordain Women." *New York Times,* 8 August 2011.

Gutierrez, Gustavo. *A Theology of Liberation: History, Politics, and Salvation.* Maryknoll: Orbis, 1973.

Healthline. "Unhappiness by the Numbers: 2012 Depression Statistics." Web. 2014.

Horton, Miles, with Herbert and Judith Kohl. *The Long Haul: An Autobiography.* New York: Doubleday, 1990.

Johnson, James Weldon, "Lift Every Voice and Sing." 1900. *The New Century Hymnal.* Cleveland: Pilgrim, 1995.

Jordan, Clarence. *The Cottonpatch Gospel: Luke and Acts.* Cited in Alan Culpepper. "The Gospel of Luke." *The New Interpreters Bible.* Vol. 9. Nashville: Abingdon, 2003.

King, Martin Luther, Jr. "I Have a Dream." 1963. *Historic Speeches of African Americans.* Ed. Warren J. Halliburton. New York: Franklin Watts, 1993.

---. "Letter from Birmingham Jail." 1963. *Why We Can't Wait.* New York: Penguin, 1964.

Klotz, Neil Douglas. *Prayers of the Cosmos: Meditations on the Aramaic Words of Jesus.* New York: Harper and Row, 1990.

Lawrence, Jerome, and Robert E. Lee. *Inherit the Wind.* New York: Ballantine, 1955.

Lazarus, Emma. "The New Colossus." 1883. *Selected Poems.* New York: Library of America, 2000.

Lorde, Audre. *The Cancer Journals, Special Edition.* San Francisco: Aunt Lute, 1997.

Manz, Paul. "E'en So, Lord Jesus, Quickly Come." St. Louis: Concordia, 1954.

McKissack, Patricia C. and Fredrick. *Sojourner Truth: Ain't I a Woman?* Jefferson City: Scholastic, 1992.

McLaren, Brian, *Finding Our Way Again: The Return of the Ancient Practices.* Nashville: Thomas Nelson, 2008.

Metzger, Deena. "In Her Own Image." *Heresies* 1, May 1977.

Moir, Anne, and David Jessel. *Brain Sex: The Real Difference Between Men and Women.* New York: Dell, 1989.

Mollenkott, Virginia. *Omnigender: A Trans-Religious Approach.* Cleveland: Pilgrim, 2001.

More, Thomas. *Utopia.* London: Penguin, 1983.

National Institute of Mental Health. "Depression in Children and Adolescents Fact Sheet." Web. 2014.

New Oxford Annotated Bible with Apocrypha: *New Revised Standard Version.* New York: Oxford University Press, 2001.

Nietzsche, Friedrich Wilhelm. *Ecce Homo.* New York: Courier Dover, 2004.

Nouwen, Henri J. M. *Can You Drink the Cup?* Notre Dame: Ave Maria, 1996.

---. *!Gracias! A Latin-American Journal.* New York: Harper & Row, 1983.

Palmer, Parker J. *Let Your Life Speak: Listening for the Voice of Vocation.* New York: Jossey-Bass, 2000.

Peterson, Eugene H. *The Message: The Bible in Contemporary Language.* Colorado Springs: NavPress, 2002.

Plato. *The Republic.* London: Penguin, 2006.

Reay, Lewis. Personal conversation. Edinburgh, Scotland. October 2009.

Reese, Florence Patton. "Which Side Are You On?" 1932.

Robinson, Kim Stanley. *Pacific Edge: Three Californias.* New York: Orb, 1995.

Roy, Arundhati. *The God of Small Things.* New York: HarperCollins, 1997.

Scott, Lesbia. "I Sing a Song of the Saints of God." *Everyday Hymns for Little Children.* London: Society of Saints Peter and Paul, 1929.

Seelye, Katharine Q. "Writer Tends Land Where Ancestors Were Slaves." *New York Times,* 20 October 2010.

Soelle, Dorothee. *Against the Wind: Memoir of a Radical Christian.* Minneapolis: Augsburg Fortress, 1999.

---. *The Silent Cry: Mysticism and Resistance.* Minneapolis: Augsburg Fortress, 2001.

---. *Strength of the Weak.* Westminster John Knox: Philadelphia, 1984.

---. *Suffering.* Minneapolis: Augsburg Fortress, 1975.

Stein, Joseph. *Fiddler on the Roof.* New York: Music Theatre International, 1964.

Stevens, Marsha. "For Those Tears I Died." *I Still Have a Dream.* Los Angeles: BALM, 1993. CD.

Stokell, Ian. "Conference Continues 2011's Assault on LGBT Bullying." *San Diego LGBT Weekly,* 15 December 2011. Web. 2014.

Teresa, Mother, and Brian Kolodiejchuk. *Mother Teresa: Come Be My Light.* New York: Doubleday, 2007.

Thompson, Will. "Softly and Tenderly." 1880. *The New Century Hymnal.* Cleveland: Pilgrim, 1995.

Thurman, Howard. *Footprints of a Dream: The Story of the Church for the Fellowship of All Peoples.* New York: Harper & Brothers, 1959.

---. Morehouse College Leadership Center. Web. 2010.

Twelve Steps and Twelve Traditions. New York: Alcoholics Anonymous World Service, 1952.

United Methodist Book of Worship. Nashville: United Methodist, 1992.

Weil, Simone. *Intimations of Christianity Among the Ancient Greeks.* 1957. Cited in Dorothee Soelle. *Suffering.* Op. cit.

Wells, H. G. *The Time Machine.* London: Heinemann, 1895.

Wesley, Charles. "Christ the Lord is Ris'n Today." 1739. *The New Century Hymnal.* Cleveland: Pilgrim, 1995.

Winter, Miriam Therese. "My Soul Gives Glory to My God." 1987. *The New Century Hymnal.* Ibid.

Williams, Miller. "Compassion." *The Ways We Touch.* Urbana: University of Illinois Press, 1997.

Yee, James, and Aimee Malloy. *For God and Country: Faith and Patriotism Under Fire.* New York: PublicAffairs, 2005.